Problem People

Dr Peter Honey is a chartered psychologist and management consultant. He worked for Ford Motor Company and British Airways before becoming freelance in 1969. He specialises in anything to do with human behaviour and its consequences, and divides his time between designing and running training programmes, consultancy assignments, and writing.

He has written widely on behavioural topics in over 50 publications. His books include *Improve Your People Skills*, *Face to Face Skills*, and *101 Ways to Develop Your People, without really trying!* His manuals, produced with Professor Alan Mumford, include *Manual of Learning Styles* and *Manual of Learning Opportunities*. He has also advised on the contents of many training films, written the accompanying booklets and appeared in the Video Arts production *Talking about Behaviour*.

He is visiting professor of managerial learning at the International Management Centre, a fellow of the Institute of Management Consultants and the Institute of Personnel and Development, a chartered psychologist with the British Psychological Society and a member of the Association for Management Education and Development. He is married, has four children, and lives in Berkshire.

Problem People

and how to manage them

Peter Honey

Institute of Personnel and Development

To David, aged 6. Never stubborn, just tenacious!

Typeset by The Comp-Room, Aylesbury
Printed in Great Britain by The Cromwell Press, Wiltshire

British Library Cataloguing-in-Publication Data

A catalogue record for this book is available from the
British Library

ISBN 0-85292-495-X

The views expressed in this book are the author's own, and may not
necessarily reflect those of the IPD.

INSTITUTE OF PERSONNEL
AND DEVELOPMENT

IPD House, Camp Road, London SW19 4UX
Tel: 0181 971 9000   Fax: 0181 263 3333
Registered office as above. Registered Charity No. 1038333
A company limited by guarantee. Registered in England No. 2931892

Contents

Acknowledgements

Thanks to:

- Sheldon Press for allowing me to reproduce a version of the question-naire that I originally compiled for *Solving Your Personal Problems*
- Suzanne Hill for masses of encouragement (and word-processing!)
- Carol Honey and our children for putting up with me while I wrote another book

Introducing problem people and people problems

We all know some problem people: bosses who are inconsistent and keep moving the goal posts; uncooperative colleagues upon whom we depend for essential services; subordinates who aren't quality conscious and fail to do things as well as we do them ourselves. Problem people aren't confined to the world of work. The train home is cancelled because the driver failed to show up. Your partner is grumpy after a frustrating day. The kids are complaining because their teacher kept them in at playtime. The builder who is extending your house has put a doorway in the wrong place.

Problem people, if it isn't too much of a tautology, give us people problems. If you think of a problem, any problem, as the difference between what you've got now and what you want, then a people problem is the difference between the behaviour you've got now and the behaviour you want. The problem person is the person whose behaviour is giving you a problem.

The emphasis on behaviour is of course intentional. What people say and what people do (or don't do!) create people problems. In fact the only way to recognise people problems is by noticing something you regard as unsatisfactory about someone's behaviour. Later we shall see that this simple truth has considerable implications.

People problems, like people themselves, come in all shapes and sizes. There are big ones so daunting that we are at a loss to see what to do to improve the situation. There are small ones that are easy to shrug off but none the less irritate. There are temporary problems that come and go without us necessarily doing anything about them. There are

1

seemingly never-ending problems that appear to be fixtures for years to come.

If problem people give you people problems, then this makes you the problem owner. The idea of 'owning' people problems, in the same way that you'd own a poodle or a house, often strikes people as unusual. But, as we shall see, it is a helpful concept when it comes to taking responsibility for our problems rather than sitting back and blaming the problem person.

It would be understandable if you have gained the impression from what I have said that other people cause your problems. Already the finger has been pointed at bosses, colleagues, subordinates, train drivers, partners, kids and builders. Yet now I am suggesting you might be a sort of Jekyll and Hyde character, both problem person and the problem owner at the same time!

The truth is that people problems are usually six of one and half a dozen of the other. This is because behaviour breeds behaviour. Through your behaviour you may, quite unintentionally, be triggering a behaviour pattern in someone else that is for you a problem. It is fascinating to see how often we unwittingly create our own people problems. Our boss might be inconsistent because we keep interrupting him or her at odd times with queries. Colleagues might be uncooperative because we failed to consult them about some essential service we required. Our subordinates might not do things to the required standards because we haven't made the standards clear.

Do people problems really matter?

There is a tendency for busy people to dismiss people problems as trivial. They are seen as matters of style not of substance. Substance is the cost-to-income ratio, or the diversification strategy, or the new marketing campaign, or the company car policy. In each case it is the *content* and not the *behaviour* that apparently enjoys the limelight. And yet my experience is that with a little encouragement (and sometimes with no encouragement) people open up about the trials and tribulations of their people problems. Their boss is driving them scatty. They are frustrated by their negative colleagues and angry about their subordinates' mistakes. It is as though substantive content issues top the *official* agenda, while substantive behavioural issues top the *hidden* agenda.

People problems matter because they:

- **waste time (and therefore money).** People grumble, gripe and speculate instead of being productive.
- **create unnecessary stress.** People upset themselves about people problems and therefore experience negative feelings that often result in displays of bad temper, absenteeism, low morale, staff attrition, and a whole plethora of unwanted side-effects.
- **distort decisions.** People problems have a nasty habit of 'contaminating' decisions as problem people are circumvented, promoted, moved sideways. Organisational structures and working practices are often designed to accommodate, appease or marginalise problem people.

That's the bad news. The good news is that people problems:

- **make life more interesting.** Each problem acts as a stimulant. This is especially true if you are the sort of person who insists that there are no problems only challenges. Life without problems would be bland and tedious.
- **provide splendid learning opportunities.** There is much to learn from analysing people problems, working out how best to solve them and monitoring successes and failures.
- **test your people skills.** Managing people who are compliant, positive and cooperative is easy. The real test of your prowess at handling people comes when you have people problems to solve. If you can manage difficult people, you can manage anybody.

Basic assumptions about problem people

Inevitably this book is based on some assumptions which it is best to declare at the outset. Check whether you agree with the following:

1 **There is no such thing as a problem person, only problem behaviours.**
   No matter what the problem is, it is never the whole person who is at fault (even though in your exasperation it might sometimes seem like it!). It is always some aspect of the person's behaviour that gives you a problem.
2 **All problem behaviours are 'made not born'.**
   This coupled with the first assumption, underpins the whole of this

3

book. If problem behaviours have been acquired, then it makes them amenable to modification. Learned behaviours can be unlearned, relearned, replaced, supplemented and so on. They are malleable rather than fixed and immutable.

3 **All problem behaviours fall into one of two categories: you are suffering from either too much or too little behaviour.** When people behave in extroverted and/or aggressive ways you have too much behaviour and need to find ways to tone it down. When people behave in introverted and/or submissive ways you have too little behaviour and need to beef it up.

4 **Problem behaviours have to be viewed situationally.** This is partly because a problem is only a problem within a given set of circumstances and partly because problems are often brought about by the situation itself.

5 **Different approaches are needed depending on whether the problem behaviour is a 'one-off' or is habitual.** It is obviously easier to nip new problems in the bud than it is to shift habitual behaviours that have settled down into a stubborn pattern. Clearly different techniques are appropriate for solving problems that have arisen only once or twice as opposed to those that have occurred many times.

About the problems in this book

This book focuses on 50 'everyday' people problems. They appear in alphabetical order and the index contains a mini-thesaurus to help you locate problems that are troubling you.

Each section explores a number of options. The options (introduced more fully in Section 3) contain ideas to consider before you get to the stage of initiating disciplinary proceedings or firing people. The ideas are offered as thought-provokers and do not pretend to be ready-made solutions. If you are expecting answers served up on a plate you will be disappointed. What works in one situation will not in another. Feasible courses of action for you depend on the nature of the problem, its urgency, your relationship with the problem person, your power to influence the situation and many other factors.

Some problems do not feature in this book at all because they are best left to the experts. For example problems of drug abuse, alcoholism, chronic depression and other clinical illnesses have deliberately been excluded. Instead, the book concentrates on behavioural problems that we all encounter from time to time. An attempt has been made to strike a balance between the generic and the specific. Some problem classifications are too global. Catch-all terms such as uncommunicative, tiresome and negative are too imprecise to be helpful. Each has to be broken down into the manifest behaviours that lead us to conclude that someone is uncommunicative or useless or untrustworthy. In fact, pinpointing the problem is one of the important skills of a problem solver. The vaguer the problem, the more uncertain you will be about how you might tackle it.

Are you a good problem owner/solver?

When you are being inconvenienced by the behaviour of a problem person it is easy to put all your energy into complaining and blaming. From your point of view you are the innocent victim and the problem person is at fault. However, you are the one with the problem and it is up to you to do something to improve the situation. Some people seem better able to accept that they are responsible for their problems than others. The checklist that follows will help you to assess the extent to which you are a good problem owner. The checklist contains 50 paired items. Simply tick the appropriate box to indicate which statement you agree with. Whenever you are not sure, leave both boxes blank. The checklist items are listed randomly so please do not assume any order of importance. For best results do this as honestly as you can rather than merely ticking the statement you think is preferable!

1 I expect everyone to like me.   A ☐ B ☐   I expect at least half the people I meet to disapprove of me.

2 When I've got a problem with someone I look to see what I did to cause it.   A ☐ B ☐   When I've got a problem with someone I blame them for causing it.

3 In my opinion people's behaviour is largely governed by their personality make-up.   A ☐ B ☐   In my opinion people's behaviour is largely governed by what happens to them.

4 I readily accept that I   A   B   Quite honestly, I think other
need to change my   □□   people need to change to
behaviour in order to   fall in line with me.
bring about changes in
other people's.

5 I must admit that I   A   B   I have a reputation for
rarely give a thought to   □□   being the sort of person
how other people are   who can sense how other
feeling.   people are feeling.

6 I'm always interested in   A   B   I think it's rather unhealthy
knowing my own   □□   to dwell on your own
shortcomings.   shortcomings.

7 When I'm sorting out a   A   B   When I'm sorting out a
problem someone is   □□   problem I try to ensure that
bound to get hurt.   everyone benefits.

8 I maintain that people   A   B   I maintain that people
acquire most of their   □□   inherit most of their
characteristic ways of   characteristic ways of
feeling and behaving.   feeling and behaving.

9 I often ask for outside   A   B   I much prefer to keep my
help when I've got a   □□   problems to myself.
problem to solve.

10 I often take a risk and try   A   B   Before I do something I like
something challenging   □□   to be fairly certain that it
or ambitious.   will be successful.

11 When people problems   A   B   When people problems crop
crop up they always   □□   up I accept them as
seem to catch me   inevitable.
unawares.

12 I often slow my   A   B   It never occurs to me to
thoughts down to check   □□   check my thoughts.
my 'inner dialogue'.

13 I'm happy to take risks   A   B   I avoid doing anything that
     so long as I have   □   □   could aggravate the
     anticipated the worst   problem and make it worse.
     that could go wrong.

14 I'm convinced that the   A   B   I reckon the best way to
     best way to change   □   □   change people's behaviour
     people's behaviour is to   is to change the events that
     change their underlying   surround it.
     attitudes.

15 There is no point in   A   B   I find that a thought-through
     planning because I chop   □   □   plan helps me to be
     and change as the mood   consistent.
     takes me.

16 In my enthusiasm I   A   B   I'm careful to be realistic
     often set off with the   □   □   and check that a solution to
     best of intentions, only   a problem is feasible before
     to find that I was too   committing myself to it.
     ambitious.

17 Other people cause me   A   B   I cause my own problems.
     problems.   □   □

18 I keep my people   A   B   I openly admit to having
     problems to myself.   □   □   people problems.

19 I don't expect people to   A   B   I expect people to change
     change as a result of   □   □   after I have had a go at
     being told they should.   them.

20 I believe that people   A   B   I reckon people are
     tend to adopt behaviour   □   □   unpredictable and react
     patterns that get them   spontaneously as the mood
     what they want.   takes them.

21 I'm always expecting to   A   B   I believe each problem is
     find ready-made   □   □   unique and needs its own
     solutions.   tailor-made solution.

22 When people criticise   A   B   When people criticise me I
me I accept it as useful   defend myself or hit back
feedback from which I   by criticising them.
stand to learn.

23 When it comes to   A   B   When it comes to solving
solving entrenched   entrenched people
people problems, I   problems, I expect
expect the results to be   immediate improvements.
gradual.

24 If you are going to level   A   B   If you are going to level
with a person I think it's   with a person, I think it's
best to strike while the   best to choose a time after
iron is hot (i.e. when the   the incident when they are
problem occurs).   likely to be more receptive.

25 I believe that I am the   A   B   I believe it is other people
only person who can   who make me feel uptight
make me feel uptight or   or angry.
angry.

26 I regularly and frequently   A   B   I never use a relaxation
use a specific relaxation   technique.
technique.

27 I rarely show sympathy   A   B   I often say things like 'I
for other people.   understand how you must
      feel . . .'

28 I believe it is best to   A   B   I believe it is best not to
suppress bad feelings.   have bad feelings.

29 People have to accept   A   B   I constantly monitor the
me as they find me.   effect my behaviour is
      having on other people.

30 I believe my head   A   B   I believe my heart should
should rule my heart.   rule my head.

31 I encourage people to comment on how well or how badly I do things.   A   B   I never ask people for personal comments – they can keep their opinions to themselves.

32 I'm often accused of putting my foot in it and unnecessarily upsetting people.   A   B   I'm careful to trim my behaviour so that it is appropriate to those I am with.

33 I stick to my strategy for solving problems despite some initial setbacks.   A   B   I easily become disheartened and give up.

34 When I've worked out what to do to solve a problem, I like to keep my strategy to myself.   A   B   When I've worked out what to do to solve a problem, I like to declare my strategy to all those involved.

35 When I've got a people problem, I believe it is best to take some initiative to prevent the problem developing.   A   B   When I've got a people problem, I think it is best to delay and see if the problem blows over.

36 When people behave in ways that disappoint me, I try to speculate about their underlying motives, attitudes and feelings.   A   B   When people behave in ways that disappoint me, I try to identify what circumstances brought about their behaviour.

37 When something goes wrong I blame others.   A   B   When something goes wrong I take responsibility.

38 I believe that people are able to choose how they feel.   A   B   I believe that emotions just happen and can't be controlled.

39 When I try to describe people problems, I find it difficult to know where to start. A ☐ B ☐ I put effort into being able to describe people problems succinctly.

40 I aim to change people's behaviour. A ☐ B ☐ I aim to change people's attitudes.

41 I refuse to accept that any problem is insoluble. A ☐ B ☐ I'm convinced that some problems are impossible to solve.

42 When I've got a people problem, I tend to get steamed up and emotional about it. A ☐ B ☐ When I've got a people problem, I like to think it over rationally.

43 When I've got a problem with someone, they are likely to be the last to know. A ☐ B ☐ When I've got a problem with someone, likely as not I'll tell them so.

44 I maintain it is best to shrug off people problems. A ☐ B ☐ I maintain it is best to face people problems squarely.

45 The bigger the problem, the more I try to break it down into manageable bits. A ☐ B ☐ The bigger the problem, the more I feel overwhelmed and uncertain where to make a start.

46 I like to trace a people problem back to its origins. A ☐ B ☐ I concentrate on under-standing the problem in the 'here-and-now'.

47 If things don't work out, I feel dejected and tend to give up. A ☐ B ☐ If things don't work out, I go back to square one and start all over again.

48 I prefer to work out my own solution to a problem and implement it quietly without any fuss.

A ☐ B ☐

I prefer to involve the problem person in planning the stategy for solving the problem.

49 On balance I prefer to reward the right behaviour.

A ☐ B ☐

On balance I prefer to punish the wrong behaviour.

50 I like to experiment with new or different ways of doing things.

A ☐ B ☐

I prefer to stick to my normal way of doing things.

How to score

Of the 50 items in the checklist, half probe your beliefs and half your actions. The first thing you need to do is 'unscramble' the items by indicating which boxes you ticked and totalling the resultant score.

Beliefs			Actions		
Item	Points		Item	Points	
	A	B		A	B
1	0	1	2	1	0
3	0	1	7	0	1
4	1	0	9	1	0
5	0	1	10	1	0
6	1	0	12	1	0
8	1	0	13	1	0
11	0	1	15	0	1
14	0	1	16	0	1
17	0	1	18	0	1
19	1	0	22	1	0
20	1	0	26	1	0
21	0	1	27	0	1
23	1	0	29	0	1
24	0	1	31	1	0
25	1	0	32	0	1
28	0	1	33	1	0

Beliefs				Actions		
Item	Points			Item	Points	
	A	B			A	B
30	1	0		34	0	1
35	1	0		36	0	1
38	1	0		37	0	1
40	1	0		39	0	1
41	1	0		42	0	1
44	0	1		43	0	1
47	0	1		45	1	0
49	1	0		46	0	1
50	1	0		48	0	1

The interpretation of your questionnaire scores is as follows:

Beliefs	Actions	Interpretation
Under 15	Under 15	You have much to learn about being a good problem owner and a successful problem solver. This book is essential reading for you!
15–20	15–20	You are already moderately good at owning and solving people problems. This book will help you to improve.
Over 20	Over 20	You are already a competent problem owner/solver. This book will help you to become even better.
Under 15	Over 20	Your techniques are good but you need to improve your grasp of the principles.
Over 20	Under 15	You've got the principles straight but you need to improve on your techniques.
15–20	Over 20	You only need to polish up on the principles.
Over 20	15–20	You only need to make some minor adjustments to your techniques.

Portrait of a successful problem owner/solver

One of the first things you'd notice about successful problem owners/
solvers is how alert they are to people problems. They readily admit to
having problems of their own and have an uncanny knack of sensing
problems that are troubling people they meet. When they describe their
people problems they do so in a succinct, matter-of-fact way. They are
not emotional or defeatist. They do not grumble or attribute blame.
Instead, they acknowledge their ownership of the problem and accept
full responsibility for doing something about it. If you tell them about a
problem which is troubling you (and this is highly likely since they are
the sort of people you find it easy to open up to) they listen more than
they talk. They ask questions about your problems and get to the heart
of the matter and, even though they haven't told you what to do, you
emerge with a clearer mind and resolved to tackle the problem. If they
proffer advice, they do so in a non-interfering, take-it-or-leave-it way.
By no stretch of the imagination are they busybodies or do-gooders.

They accept, in a passive yet positive way, the inevitability of people
problems, and expect no more than brief respites between problems.
They obviously don't *welcome* people problems, but they don't dread
them either. This mature stance helps them to detect problems at an
early stage – well before things become dire or reach a crisis point.
Once they have spotted a people problem they do not procrastinate,
hoping it will go away of its own accord. Nor do they leap into ill-considered action. Instead they think about the problem and how best to
tackle it. If they decide to use someone as a sounding-board they put
some effort into making it clear whether they want sympathy, guidance
or counselling. If they feel out of their depth they do not hesitate to
seek appropriate professional help. In doing so they harbour no illu-
sions about perfect answers and resist the temptation to shift the
responsibility for their problem on to an expert.

Healthy optimism in an outstanding characteristic of successful
problem solvers. They refuse to let people problems get them down.
They don't exactly *thrive* on problems, but when they occur they certainly view them as challenges and refuse to accept that any problem,
however horrendous or apparently intractable, is insoluble. They
believe that problems are there to be solved and that they have not just
one but many possible courses of action open to them.

Their optimism stems from two basic operating assumptions. First,
they believe that human behaviour is caused as much by external factors

as by internal 'personality' factors. Secondly, they believe that changes in external factors will inevitably result in changes in behaviour.

Successful problem solvers are confident that a thorough examination of the situation will lead to feasible ideas about how to change the behaviour in question. They are happy to apply the same systematic approach to changing their own behaviour, and fully acknowledge that they must change themselves in order to bring about beneficial changes in other people. They resist the temptation to make sweeping generalisations about people or to label personality types. Instead, they put effort into accurately observing how people are actually behaving, fully accepting and respecting differences between people. They also concentrate on what is happening in the 'here-and-now' rather than being dragged backwards into past history.

Successful problem solvers are open and honest, not just about their problems but also about their tactics. They go out of their way to 'grasp the nettle' and level with people in a non-judgemental way that doesn't cause offence. They are careful to help people to see the benefits of making changes and wary of the dangers of exploitation and manipulation.

Perhaps the most impressive characteristic of successful problem solvers is their willingness to manage their own behaviour and emotions. They are happy to experiment with themselves in a bid to learn from experience, overcome their weaknesses and develop their strengths. They both welcome and solicit feedback from other people. They readily assume that they are at fault when they experience disappointments with other people – not in any morbid or introspective way but pragmatically in the sure knowledge that they can take action to overcome the problem. They don't hesitate to confide in colleagues and to enlist help in banishing problem behaviours.

They are fascinated by the process of improving themselves, not in an earnest or obsessional way but rather with the disarming curiosity of a child at play. They are the first to laugh at themselves and the fixes they get into. They rarely show anger, boredom, depression, guilt, hurt, inadequacy, inhibition, jealousy or worry, and when they do they quickly take corrective action. Even more significantly, they rarely *feel* any of these emotions even though they deliberately expose themselves to testing situations. Accordingly, you won't find them ranting and raving, or being withdrawn and moody, or being listless and purposeless, or lamenting over past mistakes, or being non-assertive and embarrassed, or being cautious and resistant to change, or being suspicious and possessive, or wasting time worrying about the future. Instead you will find them being considerate, alert, enthusiastic, active, observant, experimenting, trustful, open and confident.

Successful problem solvers are clear that they are accountable to others for their behaviour but to themselves for their emotions.

This utopian, even pious, portrait is not intended to trigger feelings of inadequacy but rather to intrigue and excite you, to encourage you to become an even better problem owner/solver than you are at present. Clearly, the ultimate aim is to become better at solving people problems with the minimum of hassle and aggravation; but there is much else to be gained from the process. It is one of those quests, like so many in life, where the journey itself is worth savouring as much as arriving at the destination.

Problem people: the options

Short of getting rid of the problem person, there are really only four options open to you:

- do nothing
- alter your perception of the problem
- persuade the problem person to change
- modify the situation

Let us examine each one of these in turn.

▶ Do nothing

Doing nothing is always an option worth considering because sometimes something fortuitous happens to solve the problem for us. Generally speaking, however, it is an ostrich-like reaction that allows time for the problem to become bigger and more entrenched than it was originally.

There are obviously many reasons why doing nothing is an attractive option. There are plenty of excuses for not grasping the nettle. We don't want to upset people. The time is never right. Maybe it won't happen again. The fact is that doing something always involves risk, and taking a risk requires courage. How *much* courage depends on the magnitude of the risk of course, but inevitably courage is involved. We have to steel ourselves to forsake what is familiar and to face the unknown.

Hanging on to the familiar, problem people and all, is a perfectly understandable reaction. It's our way of avoiding the uncertainty of taking action or doing something different. Being in a state of uncertainty is psychologically uncomfortable, so it is predictable that we'll often be tempted to take no action and achieve psychological comfort by insisting that we did the right thing. The tendency to rationalise is an important psychological protector.

Another reason why we opt to do nothing when faced with people problems is that there is always a sporting chance that something will happen to resolve the situation. I expect you can remember times when your procrastination paid off because someone else took the initiative while you were still thinking about it. This happens to me quite frequently when I draw up a weekly, or daily, list of things to do. Often I hesitate to phone someone, or to organise something, even though it's on my list and, lo and behold, the other person contacts me, thus saving me the effort and reducing my telephone bill! It's also very satisfying to cross things off my list as 'done' even though I didn't in fact do anything!

Much the same can happen with people problems. Things do sometimes happen fortuitously and circumstances do change without us necessarily having to pluck up our courage, make a decision and implement it. The more this occurs, the more our tendency to 'wait and see' is reinforced and the more likely we are to repeat it.

Unfortunately, even though doing nothing is so understandable, and so popular, it often only succeeds in allowing people problems to get worse rather than better. People problems tend to develop incrementally and procrastination gives the problem time to grow, from something relatively minor and easy to correct to something major and difficult to tackle. The irony is that the more substantial the problem, the more risk is involved in doing something about it, and therefore the more likely we are to do nothing. This is the first of many vicious circles that we will meet as we analyse people problems in more depth.

▶ Alter your perception of the problem

Problems are always in the eye of the beholder. A major problem for one person is a minor irritation for another. A problem that overwhelms one person is accepted as a challenge by another. It follows, therefore, that your perception of the problem could, quite literally, be the problem! I admit that this is hard to accept particularly if you are suffering from an over-demanding boss, or uncooperative colleagues, or unreliable subordinates. It is even harder to accept if fellow sufferers share your perception! This seems to confirm that you must be seeing the problem correctly.

Reality is always prey to the distortions of our perceptions. The very same behaviour can be regarded in one situation as an asset and in another as a problem. Someone who talks a lot could, for example, be a welcome companion when you want to sit back and listen but a menace in a meeting where you've got something important to say but can't get a word in edgeways.

As we said earlier a people problem is the difference between the behaviour you've got and the behaviour you want. The problem is therefore how best to close the gap and remove the difference. You have two choices: either you can move the behaviour from what it is now to what you want, or you can move what you want to the behaviour you've got. Most of this book concentrates on the former, but it is always worth considering the feasibility of the latter.

What we want is based on our values and beliefs about what *should* happen. I emphasise the world 'should' quite deliberately because it is the key to understanding how our beliefs cause us to perceive problems. If, for example, I believe that my boss should always support me in front of others, then I am likely to get upset and perceive his or her behaviour to be a problem when they contradict or criticise me in public. I see the problem because of the mis-match between the actual behaviour and what I believe it *should always* be.

The key to not seeing a problem (and not becoming upset) is to change our beliefs about what should happen. For example we could believe that:

- bosses are first and foremost 'seekers after truth' and if that means correcting us in public, so be it
- bosses are providers of learning opportunities and we have much to learn from feedback, especially when it is critical
- bosses who are open, honest and straightforward are preferable to bosses who are two-faced or over diplomatic.

Any of these beliefs would reduce the gap by moving our wants towards what we've got. Clearly it isn't easy to shift deep-seated beliefs that we might have held for a long time. But all our beliefs have been acquired as we learned from previous experiences and they can therefore be 'unacquired' and updated as we learn from new experiences. That's the whole point of continuous learning.

▶ Persuade the problem person to change

This option includes a number of different approaches such as giving the person feedback, persuading them to change their behaviour, and coaching, counselling or training them. In each case the problem person's behaviour is the focus of attention and, in their different ways, each approach is aimed at helping the problem person to accept the need for change and to make the required change.

There is no doubt that these approaches, either individually or in combination, are worth a try. Often problem people are unaware that some aspect of their behaviour is for someone else a problem. The very act of pointing it out may be sufficient. More often, however, changes in behaviour, particularly if the behaviour in question has become habitual, requires more effort than a quiet word. Persuading the problem person invariably involves getting them to accept the need for change but even when this is achieved it doesn't guarantee that the behaviour in question will change. Increased awareness and intellectual acceptance, while useful, are rarely enough. This is because behaviours have been acquired through practice, sometimes over many years, and further practice is required to unlearn a problem behaviour and replace it with something better. Just as a golfer who has acquired bad habits with his swing needs feedback and painstaking practice to make the necessary adjustments to his technique, so problem people need support and encouragement as they struggle to replace the problem behaviour with another one.

So simply telling someone to change is rarely adequate. Persuading someone that it is worth while is a useful prerequisite. Counselling results in a feasible plan to change, and that is obviously helpful. Coaching and training, especially on the job, offer invaluable on-going support as the person acquires the new behaviour through trial and error.

▶ Modify the situation

This approach focuses less on the problem person and more on the situation in which the problem behaviour is occurring. Problem behaviours never 'just happen', they are always a product not just of the person but of circumstances. Something always happens to trigger the problem behaviour and something else happens often enough to reinforce it. This approach therefore examines the 'befores and afters' surrounding a behaviour to see what could be modified to trigger and reinforce something more satisfactory. Change the situation and you change the behaviour. An example will help to illustrate how this approach could work. Suppose you are suffering from an uncooperative colleague. It is unlikely that your colleague spends every waking moment being uncooperative or that he or she inherited a disposition to be uncooperative from their parents. Much more probable is that your colleague tends to be uncooperative on certain occasions, neutral on others and cooperative on others. So the question is what causes their behaviour to vary?

First, we need to look for the triggers. What is happening immediately before our colleague is uncooperative? Examples might be that he or she:

- has just taken on a large job for another client
- is frantically trying to catch the post
- has an assistant who is unexpectedly absent today
- takes exception to our presumption that our job is more of a priority than other people's
- finds the task we are asking them to do unrewarding and tedious
- is convinced that there is a better way to accomplish the task.

Any or all of these triggers would make uncooperative behaviour likely.

Secondly, we need to look at what typically happens immediately after our colleague is uncooperative. Presumably they have 'discovered' that there are more advantages in being uncooperative than in being cooperative. So what happens after the behaviour to reinforce it? Examples might be that:

- we apologise for being a nuisance to them
- we relax our demands
- we say conciliatory or complimentary things to them such as 'Sorry I didn't realise you were so busy', or 'I know you always find a way no matter how busy you are'
- We allow ourselves to be persuaded to do it their way

21

- we make alternative arrangements and get someone else to do it
- we complain to our manager who complains to their manager and our colleague is able to 'prove' that they are too busy/need more staff.

These payoffs would tend to reinforce uncooperative behaviour.

Having examined the 'befores and afters' of the situation, this approach invites us to see how we could change the triggers to make cooperation more likely and how we could reinforce it when it occurs. Some of the triggers are outside our control, but we could change our approach (in other words our behaviour) so that it was less presumptive, and we could be more open to suggestions from the colleague about how to improve the task. If these changed triggers result in cooperative behaviour then we must be careful to reinforce it with lots of support, gratitude, and recognition.

What follows are 50 problems in alphabetical order. Each is introduced with examples and then each of the four options is explored and advice given. A word of warning however: rarely will the advice apply lock, stock and barrel to your people problem. Each problem has to be understood and dealt with taking the exact circumstances into account in rather the same way that a judge has to weigh up extenuating circumstances in a murder trial. The crime may be the same but circumstances vary from case to case. So it is with people problems. Please treat the advice that follows more as thought provokers than ready-made answers to your people problems.

Abdicator

Many people find it difficult to see where delegation ends and abdication begins. Some delegators over-delegate so far that they lose control; they never enquire about, or show any interest in, what is happening. They have in fact delegated to the point of abdication.

Delegators are clear that they have entrusted a part of their job to someone else and that they, the delegators, remain accountable. By contrast, abdicators are under the impression that they have allocated work and that, once allocated, it is no longer part of *their* job. They therefore relinquish not only responsibility and authority but also accountability. This is an illusion, as they quickly discover if something goes wrong and they are held accountable for something they know nothing about.

If you suffer from an abdicating boss it is a problem for you because you are left to your own devices without guidance or feedback. This means that you are being deprived of your basic rights to know what is expected of you, how you are doing and what you need to do to improve. This is the reverse of the problems you have at the hands of a meddling interventionist boss (see **Meddler**). It is also a problem for you because, if and when something goes wrong, abdicating bosses will blame you rather than support you (see **Buck-passer**). They feel entirely justified in heaping the blame on you because they regard it as *your* job rather than part of *their* job, for which they retained accountability.

THE OPTIONS

▶ Do nothing

While everything is progressing well, and if you are inclined to be an independent spirit, you might be tempted to do nothing to spoil the freedom of working for an abdicating boss. But you are vulnerable and unprotected. If you are a risk-taker you might be happy to gamble and remain 'uninsured'. The freedom you relish must be set against the lack of feedback and the fact that you are not getting your money's worth from your boss. You must, therefore, weigh up the advantages and disadvantages of leaving well alone.

▶ Alter your perception of the problem

Instead of regarding your boss as an abdicator you could see him or her as a trusting soul who has complete faith in you. He or she never enquires about how things are going because they operate on the basis that 'no news is good news'. Your boss doesn't merely trust you to do a good job, he or she also trusts you to *keep them informed.*

If you look at it this way, you will be more likely not to abuse the trust your boss has placed in you and to see it as *your* responsibility to keep your boss informed.

Alternatively you could see your boss as benignly absent-minded and make it your business to remind him or her of the activities you are carrying out on their behalf.

Another possibility is that you see your boss as an extraordinarily reserved person (see **Reserved**) who is too shy to enquire how things are going for fear of implying some criticism.

Of course none of these shifts in perception succeeds in converting your abdicating boss into a paragon of virtue but at least they help you to see that you need to take the initiative. This could be selective; in other words you could be free to choose what to inform your boss about and what to keep to yourself. To get full value from your boss, however, err on the side of extracting their guidance, feedback and support. These can be described as your three basic rights.

▶ Persuade the problem person to change

The assertive option would be to choose your time and place and to raise the whole issue with your boss. The best way to do this would be to have ready some recent examples of your activities and to use them as a basis for agreeing some guidelines about when your boss wishes to be kept informed, and when not.

The whole idea would be to reduce ambiguity and make explicit a *modus operandi*. It would also be a means of giving them a non-accusational reminder that they are depriving you of your three basic rights and therefore not fulfilling their obligations as a boss.

▶ Modify the situation

This option assumes that your boss is an abdicator not because of some personality defect but because circumstances are encouraging them to be so. You therefore need to examine the situation by answering two questions: *when* do they abdicate and *what do they gain* by abdicating? Triggers for abdicating could be when your boss is:

- particularly busy or under pressure
- fascinated and enthusiastic about their own work
- geographically distant from you
- distracted by the demands of less reliable subordinates

Payoffs for abdicating could be:

- less hassle
- more time to get on with other more 'interesting' things
- the absence of any adverse consequences because nothing goes wrong and they are not 'caught napping'.

If these are the triggers and payoffs then they provide useful pointers for modifying the situation to encourage the behaviour you want. You could, for example, find ways to keep your boss informed that are not enormously time-consuming. You could start by involving them in aspects of your work that you know coincide with their interests and gradually extend this to aspects that they find more threatening or less exciting. The geographical gap could be overcome with regular phone calls. These are all ideas that would be likely to trigger more involvement, interest and feedback from your boss.

It is vital to cut down on the 'punishments' and, if possible, 'reward' your boss with payoffs when he or she has shown some shift from being an abdicator towards the behaviour you want. So, with the payoffs listed above, you would have to be careful not to increase their hassle (getting involved should be a pleasant experience for them) and not to encroach on their time too much.

Absentee

Absentees make a habit of not turning up for work, invariably with illness as the excuse. In the early stages it is often difficult to distinguish between genuine cases and absenteeism. After a while it becomes clear that absence is a persistent problem and the reasons sound less and less plausible.

Depending on its frequency and extent, absenteeism can be a serious problem. Clearly the productivity of the absentee is reduced but their absence can have knock-on effects and also reduce the productivity of other interdependent people. The plain fact is that whether the effects on productivity are considerable or insignificant, absentees are reneging on an agreement to perform specific tasks and work for a requisite number of hours.

THE OPTIONS

▶ Do nothing

It is all too easy to turn a blind eye to absenteeism, particularly initially, when you may be more inclined to believe the reasons offered. However, if you do nothing it is predictable that absenteeism will increase. There is a risk that it will become endemic as people start to emulate the absentee.

▶ Alter your perception of the problem

You could see absentees as thieves stealing time from their employer. In most work places stealing tangible items is regarded as a serious misdemeanour. Stealing time, while less tangible and more difficult to prove, is no less a crime.

If you perceive absentees as thieves you will be more likely to grasp the nettle and confront the problem. Too often the treatment meted out to absentees is too lenient and in effect condones the practice.

▶ Persuade the problem person to change

Absentees always have their own reasons for staying away from work and, if you want to solve the problem by persuasion, it is important to establish what they are. Perhaps they have a situation at home which is awkward and competes with their work commitments. Perhaps they dislike their work and have some absorbing outside interest which draws them like a magnet. Perhaps they have a 'work to live' philosophy and take their commitments lightly.

It is important to establish the real reasons for absenteeism so that, having understood them, you can explore ways to reduce the 'either or' conflict. 'Either I come to work or I stay at home/go fishing etc.' If, for example, there is a recurring situation at home which requires the absentee's presence, it might be possible to agree the equivalent of a flexitime system or to make some other special arrangement.

Clearly a compromise solution might be impossible or unacceptable, in which case the consequences of continued absenteeism must be spelled out and the countdown to dismissal begun.

▶ Modify the situation

In theory absenteeism is easy to fix; you make the payoffs for coming to work greater than the payoffs for not doing so. Whether absenteeism results from a problem at home or from a desire to go fishing, it is always the case that, from the absentee's point of view, there are greater advantages in staying away than there are in coming to work.

You have two choices. Either you can concentrate on making coming to work *more attractive* or you can make not coming to work *more inconvenient* – or you can combine the two approaches. In other words you can use a carrot or a stick or both. Possible carrots are to make the work itself intrinsically more interesting or satisfying and to introduce a system of performance-related pay. Possible sticks are loss of earnings, reprimands and disciplinary proceedings.

These tactics may sound fairly obvious but there are work places where an absentee's pay is unaffected by their attendance record and where absentees are virtually welcomed back because they were so desperately missed. Such reactions reinforce the tendency to stay away from work when it suits the absentee.

Apathetic

Apathetic people are among the most difficult to deal with. As every salesperson knows it is far easier to overcome objections than it is to handle a customer who is passive and indifferent.

People who are apathetic often claim that they are being 'open-minded' but this is really a euphemism for 'Well, here I am, utterly unenthusiastic; interest me if you can!' They often sit leaning back, with their arms crossed, looking bored, waiting for someone else to take the initiative.

Apathetic people are a problem because they 'sit on the fence', acquiescing without being for or against anything. Whilst apathetic people are unlikely to resist anything (see **Quarrelsome**) they are also unlikely to support anything. This means that poor-quality decisions often go through 'on the nod' with apparent rather than real agreement. Apparent agreement is dangerous because it is likely to come apart at the seams subsequently when people backtrack. And it's no good saying 'But I thought we *agreed*!' Apathetic acquiescence is, alas, not an agreement.

THE OPTIONS

▶ **Do nothing**

This is the last thing to do when faced with apathy. It is guaranteed to leave apathetic people firmly on the fence ready later to stab you in the back when it becomes convenient to take sides. So unless it suits you to have a 'silent majority' you need to do something to get a reaction.

▶ **Alter your perception of the problem**

This is tempting but dangerous. As we have seen, it is easy to perceive apathy as agreement merely because of the absence of disagreement. But this is an illusion. Apathetic people do not make good allies.

▶ **Persuade the problem person to change**

Apathetic people can often be coaxed out of a state of detached indifference. However, if you tackle them about it, expect denial, for they will put a gloss on it and claim that they are being disinterested and impartial rather than uninterested. Insist that the effect is the same regardless of their motive and that you want them to express an opinion. Give them three choices:

- agreeing, however marginally, and saying why
- disagreeing, however marginally, and saying why
- feeling ambivalent and saying why.

This is a useful recipe to force apathetic people to 'come out' and declare themselves.

▶ **Modify the situation**

No one is apathetic all the time. *Something* must turn them on. The key is to understand what circumstances bring on apathy in the problem person so that you can see what to modify about the situation to trigger interest and even enthusiasm. Possible triggers for apathy might be:

- if the problem person is allowed to 'hide' in a group and let others do all the talking
- situations where someone else takes the lead
- situations where expectations are low and people are expecting to be bored

Payoffs for apathy might be:

- staying 'safe' while other people take the risks
- reinforcing the correctness of low expectations ('I told you so!')
- Leaving all the options open to take sides later.

The answer is to change the triggers so that apathetic people have no choice but to get involved. Even a simple modification like going round the table and making everyone declare themselves will help. Giving specific roles to apathetic people also pushes them off their fence. Put them in charge of an agenda item in a meeting, get them to take the minutes or write on the flip chart. Any active role is an antidote to their preference to be passive and let other people declare themselves.

These changes to triggers force them to display more interest and be less apathetic. This deprives them of the payoffs they enjoyed. Replace these payoffs with plenty of support to make sure involvement is a good experience for them rather than a bruising one. If they have a rough time it is predictable that, given the choice, they will slip back into apathy because it is safer.

Arrogant

Arrogant people have too high an opinion of themselves. Their conceitedness evidences itself in various ways: self-satisfaction, boastfulness, a lack of self-criticism, contempt for others and a general air of smugness and complacency. These are the sort of people who, in your less charitable moments, you hope will get their come-uppance and be taken down a peg or two.

Arrogant people are a problem for two reasons. First, they undermine and antagonise less confident people. Their 'I'm OK, you're not OK' stance sends out a message which has a demotivating effect on people. Some normally co-operative people become bolshie and resistant (see **Bolshie**) in the face of continual put-downs. Secondly, arrogant people are non-learners. They invest their energies in maintaining a cosy feeling of complacency and complacency is the biggest single enemy to the process of continuously learning from experience. Arrogant people are exactly the sort of people who are destined to have one year's experience twenty times rather than twenty years' worth of experience. It is fascinating to speculate whether arrogant people actually *feel* as arrogant as they behave. Often it must be a cover-up for inner self-doubt, otherwise it is difficult to see why arrogant people continually need to let people know how wonderful they are. No one objects to self-confidence providing it is justified, not exaggerated and not thrust down our throats.

THE OPTIONS

▶ Do nothing

If the arrogant person is merely a mild irritation then you may opt to grin and bear it. If, however, the arrogance is having a detrimental effect on the morale of other people or is a blockage to the crucial process of continuous development, then it is best not to turn a blind eye. To do so would condone misplaced conceitedness.

▶ Alter your perception of the problem

There are two obvious ways in which you could do this. First, you could see the arrogant person as genuinely self-confident and oblivious of the fact that their arrogance turns other people off. This perception would help you to see that they need only be helped to be more sensitive to the reactions of others by tempering their boastfulness and displaying more modesty. After all, self-confidence is preferable to self-doubt; it is the behaviour that needs some adjustment.

Secondly, you could see the arrogance as a show of outward bluster covering up inner feelings of inadequacy. This would help you and others to be tolerant towards boastfulness and see it as a cry for affirmation. Presumably if the arrogant person was totally confident that you thought they were wonderful they would have less need to be boastful.

▶ Persuade the problem person to change

As usual there are two stages to go through. Before the arrogant person is in a position to change their behaviour they must accept that it needs changing. Clearly getting an arrogant person to acknowledge this is in itself a tall order. The best hope is not to convince them that boastfulness is necessarily wrong but that, ironically, their tendency to boast is self-defeating. Demonstrate how it undermines their reputation and gets people to think less well of them. Argue that they don't *need* to boast, just to exude confidence without all the conceit. They may need examples from their recent experience to distinguish between behaving confidently and behaving boastfully.

The second stage, once the problem has been acknowledged, is to produce a tailor-made action plan that will help the person strike a balance between showing confidence and being conceited. An admirable plan would be to have weekly 'confessionals' where the person has to confess something they have not done as well as they might and describe how they are going to do better in future. This forces them to review their performance, something they would never do if left to their own devices (or if they did, they would never admit to it).

Another tactic worth considering is setting the arrogant person the challenge of helping someone who is characteristically meek and mild to blow their own trumpet more. This plan holds out the possibility of solving two problems in a mutually advantageous way: the arrogant person, through coaching, becomes more thoughtful about conceitedness and its effect on others; the modest person is helped to see how to be more confident and that it is OK to boast at times.

▶ Modify the situation

Even the most arrogant person is not conceited all the time – there will be times when they bite their tongue and are more circumspect. Any variance in their conceitedness gives us hope for it shows that modesty is within their repertoire. We just have to analyse in what circumstances they are most conceited to see if it gives us useful clues on how we would modify the situation to trigger more modesty.

Possible triggers for arrogance are:

- when the person feels their talents or accomplishments have been undervalued or overlooked
- when they are supervising someone less experienced
- when they have a captive audience to show off to
- when there is someone worth impressing (often an accomplished person or another arrogant person).

These triggers help us to see that arrogance is a bid to impress certain types of audience. One way to prevent displays of arrogance on these occasions is to take the initiative and sing the praises of the arrogant person in their presence. At a stroke this reduces the need for them to do so and, if you are sufficiently lavish in your praises, it may even trigger some modesty on their part. This, incidentally, is the opposite of what you might normally do: when someone arrogant is present you are more likely to avoid championing them. But this deprivation is in itself a trigger for them to be boastful. Of course arrogant people indulge in this behaviour because in their perception it works.

Payoffs for arrogance tend to be of the attention-grabbing variety:

- people listen and appear impressed
- people who would otherwise be confident give up the unequal struggle and defer to the arrogant person
- the arrogant person has left people in no doubt that he or she is wonderful.

An effective tactic is to reverse the usual state of affairs by paying less attention to the person when they are boastful and more attention to them when they are not, but it is easier said than done. Since arrogant people tend to be non-learners, it speeds up the process if you tell them you are going to do this. They will be intrigued and the realisation that you are prepared to go to such lengths may cure their boastfulness, when they are with you. More probably, they will remember for a while then slip back into their usual behaviour pattern. This is when you need to reverse their payoffs.

Authoritarian

Authoritarian people are dictatorial and bossy. They lay down the law and tell other people what to do. Their operating assumption is that people are basically lazy and can't be trusted. This means that the authoritarian believes that it is constantly necessary to make decisions for people (because no one else is capable of making them or because even if they did, they'd get it wrong). Authoritarians always know what's best for people and expect unswerving obedience.

Sometimes there are situations that demand 'strong' leadership and authoritarians then come into their own. The problem, however, is that they have a tendency to think that their style is appropriate for *every* situation. Accordingly they behave in authoritarian ways regardless of whether it is called for or not.

Authoritarians are a problem because they diminish the people they dictate to. This is the reverse of empowering people. The authoritarian talks too much and doesn't listen enough; tells too much and doesn't ask enough; disagrees too much and doesn't build enough. This tends to add up to a punitive, uncompromising regime where initiatives are not tolerated and total compliance is demanded. People who are not prepared to buckle under leave or are sacked. People who remain become lackeys. Interestingly, history has shown time and time again that while authoritarian behaviours appear to work in the short term the independent spirit will eventually come out, like a genie escaping from a bottle. Authoritarian people sustain a dictatorial stance in order to keep the genie in the bottle, yet once their backs are turned people relax and savour their freedom. It is only when the authoritarian returns that people get their heads down and that, at least on the surface, things look orderly and industrious once more.

THE OPTIONS

▶ Do nothing

If you are the sort of person who enjoys the certainty of being told what to do then do nothing. It suits many people to have someone else taking all the decisions. It absolves them of responsibility and when things go wrong they can say, 'I was only obeying orders.' If, on the other hand, you find the authoritarian person cramps your style and limits your development then you will want to do something to improve the situation.

▶ Alter your perception of the problem

There are two potentially useful ways to alter your perception. Both help to reduce your fear of the autocratic person and therefore make it more likely that you will assert yourself. First, you could view the authoritarian person not as strong but as weak. You could ask yourself why they need to be in control, lording it over other people. You could postulate that this behaviour stems from strong feelings of inadequacy. They are fearful of individual liberty because of the risk of losing control. You could reassure yourself that confident people respect individual differences and welcome initiatives. Secondly, you could concentrate on imagining the authoritarian person in some undignified posture. Sitting on the toilet does the trick for many people! This helps you to see that they are human after all.

Both these changes in perception would help you to be more tolerant and less resentful of authoritarian behaviour. One other possibility is to see your authoritarian as a benevolent autocrat who is protecting you from the wicked world for your own good. It is of course arrogant of them to assume you need protection but at least it helps you to see that their heart might be in the right place.

▶ Persuade the problem person to change

Authoritarians rarely bother to look at their behaviour from anyone else's point of view. The fact that people have different perceptions of the same thing is unpalatable to them; if other people's perceptions differ from theirs then those other people are wrong, end of story. You therefore tend to be on a hiding to nothing if you attempt to give feedback to an authoritarian. The only exception is if the feedback comes from someone the authoritarian respects and regards as credible. This usually has to be someone senior to them (authoritarians are rarely authoritarian upwards) or an uninvolved third party such as an outside management consultant or trainer. If the feedback comes from a credible source, authoritarians will often capitulate and admit to inner fears of losing control and the oppressive consequences of their style.

This increased awareness is, however, rarely sufficient to bring about a modification of their behaviour. In addition, they need practice in key behaviours that are not in their repertoire, such as listening, asking and building. Training and/or coaching can provide this but that assumes that we have got the authoritarian into 'learning mode' with a strong wish to find alternative ways of behaving.

▶ Modify the situation

Authoritarians are authoritarians because it works – or that's the way they see it. If it didn't work they would do something else. This must mean that the key to understanding authoritarian behaviour lies in the situation. Even the most rampant authoritarian varies his or her style to some extent; sometimes they are extremely bossy and at other times less so. It helps therefore to see what circumstances bring on their tyrannical behaviour and what happens to encourage its repetition. Possible triggers for authoritarian behaviour might be when:

- there is a risk of chaos, disorder, uncertainty
- a non-negotiable matter of principle is threatened or violated
- a junior or younger person is insubordinate or disobedient.

Payoffs for the authoritarian are that:

- order is restored or maintained

39

- people are deferential, obedient or compliant
- things get done the 'correct' way.

Outright rebellion is often risky, but these triggers help you to see how anything that 'rocks the boat' brings on a bout of authoritarian behaviour. You will reduce the problem if you are compliant on the issues that are sacrosanct and non-negotiable but otherwise assertive. A useful approach is to assume that it is all right to do things until told otherwise. From time to time this will get you into trouble but if you are selective and steer clear of the non-negotiable areas, you can make yourself some space for initiatives. Since the authoritarian has a low tolerance for disorder, it is important that any initiatives you take do not jeopardise the orderliness that is so crucial to them. You can go so far but no further.

Boaster

Boasters brag about their achievements and make exaggerated claims. Whereas most people tend to err on the side of modesty, boasters are conceited and forever telling people about their exploits, conquests, skills, material possessions and connections. They behave as if they are supremely confident and seem impervious to criticism and put-downs from other people.

Boastful people can be a problem because their exaggerated self-image makes them over-optimistic about what they can achieve. They rush in where angels fear to tread and, even if they come to grief, they still find plenty to boast about. They cannot bring themselves to admit to any inadequacies or to ask for help. Anything which involves an admission of fallibility is a no-go area and this severely limits their ability to learn from experience. Boasters are inclined to make the same mistake over and over again because they couldn't humble themselves to heed someone's advice or learn from other people's experience.

THE OPTIONS

▶ **Do nothing**

Boasting may be an idiosyncrasy you are prepared to live with provided it does not have an adverse affect on the boaster's performance. If it is a harmless characteristic, you could ignore it and in that way refuse to provide the admiring audience boasters relish. If you do this, boasting may well decline in your presence but increase with other people who are more appreciative. If boasting is detrimental to performance, because, say, it leads to exaggerated claims to customers that cannot realistically be met, or because conceit blinds the boastful person to the possibility of self-improvement, then doing nothing is no longer a sensible option.

▶ **Alter your perception of the problem**

You could perceive boasters as confident well-balanced people who refuse to feign modesty. Modesty is built into our culture and learning to behave modestly is part of the socialisation process. Boasters are obviously people who rebelled against this and learned to blow their own trumpets. If everyone did the same, boasting would become the norm and it wouldn't seem like boasting any more. It is the contrast between the modest and the boastful that creates the problem. Perhaps being proud and boastful is psychologically healthier than being self-deprecating and humble. After all, there are many people with low self-esteem who would greatly benefit from a bit of self-hype to bolster their confidence.

This perception may help you to regard boasting as a desirable characteristic, and to encourage you to indulge in it a bit more yourself.

▶ **Persuade the problem person to change**

The likelihood is that boasters aren't nearly as confident and secure as they appear. Why else would they boast unless it was a form of self-affirmation and to win admiration. It is insecure egos that go off on ego trips. Be careful, therefore, not to wade in too heavily, imagining that they are robust enough to take it and finish up totally deflating the boaster. Nor do you want to overdo things and get the boaster to hide their light under a bushel.

Since boasters are so keen to impress, the best approach is to accept this as a laudable objective and use it as the basis for assessing the effectiveness of boastful statements. It is best to have some recent verbatim examples ready and invite the boaster to put them in order from those most likely to impress or establish credibility to those least likely to do so. Then work through the 'most likelies' to see if they run the risk of impressing in the short term but being sustainable in the medium to long term. This could prove salutary because boasters tend to go for immediate gratification without considering the longer-term implications – for example that they can't deliver all that they boast and are bound, sooner or later, to be exposed.

All this should help the boaster to discover which remarks impress in the short term and are deliverable in the long term, and which remarks are best left unsaid because they risk antagonising people. They can continue to think boastful thoughts so long as they censor the ones that won't impress.

▶ Modify the situation

Boasting is a habitual behaviour pattern sustained by strong approving payoffs. If boasting is never reinforced, it will not become established. The answer is, therefore, to deprive boasters of their payoffs so that they gradually alter their behaviour. The most obvious tactic is to register your disapproval every time boasting occurs. This reverses the outcome boasters desire. It would help if you could enlist the co-operation of a number of people who have regular dealings with the boaster so that you all stick to the same recipe.

Another, riskier, tactic is to out-boast the boaster by matching boast for boast. This shows them how unimpressive it is and, at the same time, provides you with an excuse to sing your own praises. Who knows, with practice you might swop places with the boaster!

43

Bolshie

Bolshie people tend to be disobedient, rebellious, bloody-minded and obstructive – a depressing list! Often in conversation the bolshie person appears surly but reasonably compliant. The extent of their defiance only becomes apparent subsequently when it is revealed that they have not done what you wanted them to do. When questioned, they will often be bolshie about the very fact that they are being questioned, and fail to articulate their grievances. It is the equivalent of customers voting with their feet rather than troubling to explain why they are rebelling. Bolshie people don't necessarily *choose* actions rather than words; they often feel unable to express themselves adequately in any other way. Articulate people are more likely to verbalise their grievances and come across as grumblers (see **Whinger**).

Bolshie people are a problem because you cannot trust them to do what you need. They require a disproportionate amount of close supervision. It is also likely that their bolshieness will spread to other colleagues on the 'one rotten apple in a barrel' principle. Who knows, you could even have a full-scale mutiny on your hands!

THE OPTIONS

▶ **Do nothing**

This is the coward's way out. Bloody-mindedness puts an unacceptable blight on people's performance and rarely goes away of its own accord. Something has to be done to correct the situation.

▶ **Alter your perception of the problem**

Instead of blaming the bolshie person you could perceive their displays of bloody-mindedness as a helpful indication of the presence of a grievance that needs to be sorted out. Of course, you wish they had done the straightforward thing and raised it with you. If, however, you assume that they couldn't bring themselves to do this for some reason (perhaps, despite all your protestations to the contrary, because they find you unapproachable), then bolshieness is the only option for the inarticulate. Regarding bolshieness as the equivalent of smoke signals on the horizon provides you with a welcome early-warning system well before things escalate to mutinous proportions.

▶ **Persuade the problem person to change**

Bolshie people are not likely to respond well to appeals to 'pull their socks up' and speeches about the need for everyone to carry their weight. Such approaches assume that the bolshie person is at fault and while this may be true from your point of view, the contrary is true for them. They are quite certain that you or circumstances are to blame and that their bloody-mindedness is fully justified. So pep talks miss the point and, if anything, exacerbate bloody-mindedness.

Much more fruitful is a non-accusational exploration of the reason for their bolshieness. The skill is to get them to open up. Avoid daunting questions that put them on the spot such as 'Why are you bolshie?' (the answer tends to be either 'I'm not' or 'What do you mean?'), or 'What's the matter?' (answer: 'Nothing'). Much more useful is to think hard about when they are bolshie and to have a number of suggestions ready to get the ball rolling. Pose each suggestion as an open-ended question to make it as likely as possible that the bolshie person will be forthcoming. So questions like 'Is it the new shift pattern?' and 'Do you object to moving furniture?' are out. More promising questions are 'How does the new shift pattern affect you?' and 'What did you think about being asked to move furniture when it is not in your job description?' Bolshie people have always got reasons for their behaviour, if only we can bring them to the surface. Reducing the bolshieness then depends on your ability to modify the situation.

▶ Modify the situation

Bolshieness is definitely one of those behaviours that comes and goes. Someone may appear permanently bolshie at work and by contrast be enormously enthusiastic in following some hobby or interest outside work. The key to understanding this is, of course, the difference between mandatory and discretionary activities. In leisure time the bolshie person is free to pursue whatever interests them on a voluntary basis. They have absolute discretion. At work the reverse is true. Possible triggers for bolshie behaviour are when:

- a grievance has not been dealt with or acknowledged
- the work is boring or repetitive
- their boss is authoritarian or arrogant.

These triggers provide a useful clue to how to reduce bolshieness. The more bolshie people can be involved, rather than simply receiving instructions, the less bloody-minded they are likely to be. This is not original, nor is it magic. Bolshie people are quite likely to be bolshie about attempts to involve them, but if you persist, they will eventually get sucked in despite themselves. The other powerful change you can make is to increase their responsibilities – preferably putting them in a position where they supervise others. This may not be feasible, but if a way can be found it can certainly lead to some dramatic transformations.

Payoffs for bolshie behaviour might be when:

- they have made their point or registered their protest
- eventually someone is compelled to take notice
- concessions are won.

Bolshie people are convinced that bolshieness works, to the extent that they will even indulge in long and apparently self-defeating strikes – the ultimate rebellion. The answer is to prevent bolshieness, or at least nip it in the bud by changing the cues. Attempting to 'break' bolshie people by depriving them of their payoffs can be a protracted business and creates extra resentments that fuel long-term bolshieness. In the long run it is often wiser to risk reinforcing bolshieness by being seen to take action than to leave it festering and hope that the people concerned will conclude that bloody-mindedness does not work.

Bore

It is inevitable that some people you have dealings with will be less interesting to you than others. People you find boring clearly fall into this category. It is always worth identifying what it is about them that leads you to the conclusion that they are boring. It might be because they are:

- anecdotal, giving long accounts of things which have happened to them in the past
- repetitive, saying the same things over and over again
- egotistical, talking about themselves and showing no interest in anyone else
- not on the same wavelength, with interests and enthusiasms which don't coincide with yours
- humourless

Bores tend to tell, not ask. It is rare for bores to ask questions, and if they do they are usually rhetorical or no interest is shown in the answer. A bore is a person who talks when you want him or her to listen.

Bores are only a problem if you are stuck with them and there is no escape. Perhaps you share an office with someone you find boring or you frequently have to attend meetings with someone who drones on, grinding their own axe.

THE OPTIONS

▶ **Do nothing**

An extraordinary characteristic of many bores is that they don't require you to do anything other than be there to be talked at. Given the choice they would probably prefer that you were attentive and nodded occasionally but a real bore will chunter on without any of the usual signs of encouragement. So ignoring a bore is not likely to be an effective disincentive; they are too thick-skinned to be put off so easily.

▶ **Alter your perception of the problem**

You could persuade yourself that there is no such thing as a boring person; only people you choose to feel bored by. Putting it this way could help you to see that boredom is a reaction on your part rather than something someone else does to you. Clearly it is easier to point an accusing finger and maintain that it is the bore's fault, but this is a defeatist stance which means you are unlikely to take any responsibility for improving the situation. No one can *make* you feel bored. It is a response you *choose* to have when you are with certain people and it is up to you to do something about it.

▶ **Persuade the problem person to change**

Persuading a bore not to be boring is unlikely to bring about any lasting improvement. They will find that your perception does not match with theirs and therefore conclude that you are wrong. They will claim that since other people find them fascinating you are the odd one out. They will take the line that the bored are more contemptible than the boring. You can't win.

A more promising approach is to avoid any talk of boredom and concentrate on the imbalance between telling and asking in the bore's behaviour. They are less likely to take umbrage with a nuance like this. Challenge them during the next few conversations with you to have a ratio of one to one – as many questions as statements. Later you could progress to them asking open questions and, later still, even listening to the answers!

Small steps are more likely to be palatable and it is possible for a bore to become 'hooked' on asking questions once they have discovered them.

▶ Modify the situation

Bores enjoy the sound of their own voice and a captive audience. You could change the situation by removing yourself, and depriving the bore of their captive audience, but if they are a colleague or your boss this may not be entirely feasible. In most situations the bore is used to getting their own way; people fall silent, succumb and appear to listen. Such compliance only reinforces the boring behaviour.

There are two ways to modify boring behaviour and both involve taking the initiative rather than conceding it to the bore. First, keep asking them questions so that you control the conversation. As soon as they become anecdotal or too expansive, interrupt with the next question and so on. It's hard work but it keeps you in control and prevents the bore from hijacking the conversation. The precise questions you ask depend on your objective. If it's a casual conversation, say over lunch, you can set yourself the challenge of discovering something interesting or fascinating about the boring person. It is always possible to achieve this if you persevere.

The second tactic is to give them as good as they give and match each anecdote with one of your own. Pretend that, instead of droning on with no interest in whatever you have to say, the bore has actually asked you a question and is waiting agog for your answer. You could even start with 'I'm glad you asked me that' and see if they get the message!

The key, therefore, to changing a bore is your own behaviour. Bores are used to having the upper hand. By refusing to relinquish control you set the agenda. If you fail to do this, you will get the bores you deserve.

Buck-passer

Buck-passing happens a great deal in organisations where apportioning blame is the norm. Blaming breeds blaming. Senior management blames middle management, middle management blames junior management, junior management blames their subordinates, the night shift blames the day shift, manufacturing blames product design, accounting blames management services, personnel blames the unions and the annual report blames the government and high interest rates. The name of the game is to make quite sure that the buck doesn't stop here!

For some people buck-passing has been developed to the point where it is the equivalent of a knee-jerk reaction. As soon as anything goes wrong, or as soon as there is anything resembling criticism, they immediately blame someone or something else.

If you have dealings with a blamer it is likely to be a problem for two reasons. First, you may be the person they point the finger at (and, before you realise what is happening, you might find yourself buck-passing). Secondly, blamers are notoriously difficult people to help. Blaming is their way of defending themselves, and while they are doing this they erect barriers against being helped to learn from experience. Useful maxims such as 'It isn't what you do or did, it's what you do next' and 'A good workman never blames his tools' tend to fall on deaf ears.

THE OPTIONS

▶ **Do nothing**

This is not recommended. If you do nothing, buck-passing will flourish. As we have seen it tends to be infectious and to take a hold on whole organisations very quickly. The temptation to do nothing is considerable; in fact it is in itself a form of buck-passing. Perhaps you think it is up to senior management to bring about the change. Or perhaps you are a defeatist and think buck-passing is human nature. If so, this is the ultimate in buck-passing!

▶ **Alter your perception of the problem**

Situations are always more complex than we believe at first and we tend to hanker after simplistic solutions to problems. If you assume, therefore, that each blame contains a grain of truth, it will help you to analyse complex situations and appreciate their multi-faceted nature. The trick is to track the buck as it is passed, to assume that each buck-passer is implicated, even though they all protest their innocence, and then to see how best to solve the problem taking all the factors you have discovered into account. This is likely to lead to a permanent solution rather than a 'quick fix', where many associated factors are ignored.

This change in perception will help you to learn from each buck-passer without being hoodwinked.

▶ **Persuade the problem person to change**

It is certainly worth counselling habitual buck-passers. If it has become a reflex action they may be unaware that they are doing it, and of the problems it creates for you. Raise the matter when next they slip unthinkingly into blaming behaviour.

The aim is to get them to recognise that this is what they are doing. That may well be tough because they will construe it as criticism and step up their efforts to defend themselves (see **Defensive**). Next probe to discover why they think they pass the buck. Is it because they fear retribution? Is it because they genuinely feel they are blameless? Is it because they have long standing grievances that no one acknowledges or does anything about? This probing will not solve the problem but at least it will increase their self-awareness.

Finally, concentrate on producing a feasible action plan they can use to nip buck-passing in the bud. For example they could have a formula such as 'One "I" action before one "them" blame.' Translated this means they must come up with one thing they are going to do to improve the situation *before* being allowed to blame someone else. This forces them to accept some responsibility for the situation and, after they have done that, they are less likely to put all their energy into blaming others. If they forget and blame first, then as a penance make them say two things they are going to do.

▶ **Modify the situation**

This option assumes that buck-passing is more a product of the situation than a personality trait of the person. You need, therefore, to analyse the situation surrounding buck-passing behaviour, to see if you can change any of the circumstances. Change the situation and you change the behaviour.

First, establish *when* buck-passing occurs. Examples might be when:

- the person has failed to meet a deadline
- they have been let down by other people or factors outside their control
- they are being accused
- a witch-hunt is being conducted.

Secondly, establish what happens *after* buck-passing has occurred that encourages its repetition in similar circumstances. Examples might be that:

- the person succeeds in deflecting the blame
- they demonstrate their 'innocence', and factors outside their control are entirely to blame
- the accusers retract and apologise for having misunderstood the situation
- the person succeeds in registering a point and makes a strong case for change in the system or more resources etc.

These triggers and payoffs provide thought-provokers on what it might be possible to change. For example, interim progress checks could be made long before a deadline expires and action taken to ensure that deadlines are met. You could be careful never to accuse or witch-hunt but instead to conduct regular non-accusational reviews where you are the first to admit your own shortcomings and fallibility. Whenever the buck-passer responds by accepting responsibility, you should be supportive and agree with their actions to avoid the repetition of similar events in the future. By contrast, if they persist in blaming, then you would have to ensure that they do not get away with it by depriving them of the payoffs their buck-passing usually achieves.

Bureaucrat

People with bureaucratic tendencies believe that the answer to everything is to have laid-down regulations or procedures – preferably in writing, on regulation paper, following standardised formats and in triplicate! Often they are right: rules, regulations and procedures clearly have an important part to play in many situations. They provoke people into doing things that, left to individual discretion, wouldn't otherwise get done. They also put pressure on people to do things in the same way thus fostering uniformity and standardisation.

The problem is that bureaucratic people so often overdo it and invent rules, regulations and procedures for situations where we'd be better off without them. They do this with the best of intentions, assuming that regulations are the only way to impose order on what they fear would otherwise be anarchy.

The paradox is that a surfeit of rules and regulations seems to act as a supreme challenge to so many people. People are often at their most inventive in thinking of ways to beat the system and exploit loop-holes. In rather the same way that motorways attract traffic, regulations attract ingenuity. If a regulation doesn't work, the bureaucratic person piles in with extra sub-routines and further procedures to close the loop-holes and make it foolproof. This only serves to escalate the battle between the bolshies (see **Bolshie**) and the bureaucrats.

THE OPTIONS

▶ **Do nothing**

If you do nothing about bureaucracy you will find yourself slavishly following procedures irrespective of whether or not they are serving a useful function. It is surprising how often procedures assume a life of their own and become rituals long after they have outlived their usefulness. The safest course is to challenge bureaucracy every step of the way. This is not to deny its undoubted usefulness in many situations, but to provide a counterbalance to the easy assumption that bureaucracy is always the answer.

▶ **Alter your perception of the problem**

If you regard rules, regulations and procedures as unhelpful things that cramp your style you could try perceiving them as helpful things that systematise routine for the common good and leave you free to put creative energy into more exciting ventures and the things that really matter.

Clearly the perception would be difficult to sustain if bureaucratic demands consume a disproportionate amount of your time. Try listing the things you resent but have to do because of bureaucracy, and work out the advantages to you (not to the bureaucrats). If, having searched, there is no benefit, question the appropriate bureaucrat. Even in cases where the system is unrelenting and there is no benefit to you, you could convince yourself that you are being splendidly altruistic.

▶ **Persuade the problem person to change**

You could feed back your resentment to the bureaucratic person and help them to see when rules, regulations and procedures are appropriate and when they aren't. Get them to draw up rules for when to have rules. They'll love it – the ultimate in bureaucracy!

▶ Modify the situation

Bureaucrats aren't born, they are made. Experience has taught them that regulations are the answer. As we have seen, they are often right, so it is important to target those occasions when their bureaucratic tendencies take them too far and create problems for you. Possible triggers for bureaucracy are when:

- risks (such as of creating an awkward precedent, of financial loss, to safety) are judged to be unacceptably high
- there is an apparent loss of control because people are doing their own thing
- information routinely needs to be assembled and collated centrally
- the activities of a large number of people or geographically dispersed staff need to be standardised.

Possible payoffs for bureaucratic behaviour are:

- order (as opposed to disorder)
- control of people at a distance
- clamping down on people who rebel or don't comply
- being able to say, 'It's all your fault, you should have stuck to the procedures.'

These triggers and payoffs help us to see that bureaucrats have a low tolerance for messiness and ambiguity. It is important for them to be in control. The best way to change the situation so that you are given more room for manoeuvre is to demonstrate to the bureaucrat that their expectations of disorder are unfounded. Take every opportunity to demonstrate that you are organised, things are planned, contingencies are at the ready; in short, that you have planned the 'hows', and not just the 'whats'. This will reassure them that you understand the need for order (in fact they may even consider you a fellow bureaucrat!) and that you are maximising certainty and minimising uncertainty.

Circuitous

Circuitous people love the sound of their own voices. Conversations with them tend to be discursive and rambling. They move from one point to another with no obvious planned sequence. They are rarely direct, preferring to approach subjects in an oblique, roundabout way. Often what they have to say is interesting (they are given to philosophising about this and that), but they take too long over it and are easily side-tracked.

Circuitous people are a problem in all discussions and particularly in formal meetings with a heavy agenda to get through. It is difficult to keep them to the point and to get them to be succinct and precise. Meetings with circuitous people therefore tend to go round in circles and to achieve less than, or take longer than, they should. Circuitous people rarely *intend* to filibuster or to be awkward, but even when it is innocent their behaviour is invariably disruptive.

THE OPTIONS

▶ Do nothing

It is tempting to sit back and give a circuitous person a free rein. Trying to control them takes effort; passive submission is a much easier option. But if you give an inch they will take a mile and be content to ramble indecisively and indefinitely. The whole point of a meeting is to be purposeful and achieve a worthwhile end result whether it be to have participants better informed (as in a briefing meeting) or to reach agreement (as in a problem-solving or decision-making meeting). Circuitous, discursive people make it much more difficult to reach a definitive end point. If you do nothing, it is guaranteed that meetings will take longer and longer and achieve less and less.

▶ Alter your perception of the problem

You could perceive circuitous people as thinkers who like to roam over a broad range of loosely associated issues in a bid to consider every angle and leave no stone unturned.

Since relevance is always in the eye of the beholder circuitous people may have a different understanding of the importance of issues that we see as unconnected and discursive. Admittedly it would help if they were better at demonstrating the relevance of the topics they bring up, but discursive explorations may have a useful part to play in the scheme of things. The acid test is how often a circuitous person hits the jackpot by stumbling upon an issue that other people find pertinent and worthy of an airing. If it's never, then either the circuitous person is barking up the wrong tree or other people are being too dismissive and failing to listen.

▶ Persuade the problem person to change

Circuitous people tend to be interested in a broad cross-section of subjects and to find objectives, agendas and other techniques designed to ensure that people are business-like unduly restrictive. They resent being put into what feels to them like a straitjacket. It is important to show empathy with their point of view but nonetheless to convince them that meetings need to be focused or else there is a danger that nothing will be achieved. Interesting, wide-ranging discussions may be appropriate at other times (indeed, some meetings might be specifically convened for just that purpose), but most meetings benefit from a bit of tunnel vision.

Suggest that they should never go to a meeting without knowing the objective in advance or getting an assurance that an objective will be agreed at the outset. Help them to understand that an objective describes the end result a meeting is supposed to achieve, and the more precise the description of the end result the more likely it is that participants will have a common understanding of what is relevant. The challenge for a discursive person is whether they can become self-regulating, constantly checking what they want to say for relevance against the objective. This is infinitely preferable to the chairperson having the job of keeping them to the point.

Counsel the circuitous person to check, *before* they speak, whether what they want to say will help progress towards the objective. Encourage them to make frequent and explicit references to the objectives with expressions like 'In the light of our objective I suggest . . .', 'This is relevant to the objective because . . .', 'I see a connection between the objective we are trying to achieve and . . .'. This will not guarantee that the circuitous person will never again be discursive (they might after all see connections with the objectives that are lost on everyone else), but at least it will encourage them to check for relevance before they speak.

▶ Modify the situation

There are a number of ways to change the situation so that circuitous behaviour is discouraged.

First, avoid multi-topic meetings and encourage single-topic ones. Long agendas that include a number of different topics mean the objectives become fuzzy and judgements about what is relevant are more difficult. If multi-topic meetings cannot be avoided, because, for example, participants come from different locations and it would be uneconomic to increase the number of meetings, then they should be treated as a lot of mini-meetings strung together with a clear objective for each agenda item.

Secondly, wherever possible display the objective on a flip chart or whiteboard so that it is hard to ignore and readily available for constant reference.

Thirdly, when in your judgement the circuitous person deviates, ask them to clarify how what they have said is relevant to the objective – 'What has that got to do with this objective?' Stick to this formula each time they are circuitous, thus forcing them to search for a convincing connection.

Fourthly, have an on-going 'other issues' list so that you can be seen to acknowledge and capture discursive points but then put them to one side and press on with what is relevant. At the end of the meeting, or after the meeting, go through each point on the list asking the circuitous person what, if anything, they want to do about it.

Finally, if all else fails, you could suggest that they chair the meeting. Giving them responsibility for looking after the processes of the discussion, including clarification of the objectives and keeping people to the point, works wonders. They might not chair it very well, but at least they will discover the difficulties of controlling discursive people!

Coaster

Coasters are people who free-wheel and do the minimum to get by. Classic examples are people who are approaching retirement or seeing out a period of notice. They are secure in the knowledge that dismissal, the ultimate sanction, is virtually impossible. So, they coast downhill, out of gear, with their engines ticking over effortlessly.

Coasting can be a problem because doing the minimum to get by is infectious. It has a demotivating effect on people who work with, or come into contact with, the coaster.

Coasters are often given to gloating about their impending departure and talking of little else. They enthuse about their 'escape' and, if coasting towards retirement, talk endlessly about their plans. This can have an unsettling effect on other people and stir feelings of envy as people begin to wonder if the grass on the other side *is* greener.

THE OPTIONS

▶ Do nothing

It is easy to empathise with a coaster and turn a blind eye. If they are soon to depart, what is the point of investing effort and inconveniencing yourself? In effect you elect to coast about the coaster! Coasting is rife precisely because it is so widely condoned. If you choose to do nothing, you will get less out of the coaster and allow him or her to have a detrimental effect on the performance of others.

▶ Alter your perception of the problem

Instead of thinking of coasters as benign and harmless you could perceive them as saboteurs working to undermine confidence and productivity. Why else would they spend so much time gloating instead of going quietly? Coasters would be shocked to discover that they were being regarded as saboteurs, and would no doubt protest their innocence. Nonetheless if you perceive them in this way you will be more likely to take action to combat their insidious attack.

▶ Persuade the problem person to change

The chances are that coasters are so wrapped up in their future plans that they are oblivious of the detrimental effects these plans are having on their performance. Living for the future is invariably a mistake: you miss out on the 'here-and-now' and there is no guarantee that there will be a future. Think of all the tragic cases where someone coasts towards retirement, making plans to decorate, garden, travel etc. and then drops dead before having a chance to implement their plans.

Anything you can do to persuade the coaster to concern themselves more with the present than the future will be helpful. It is conceivable that the shock tactic of accusing them of sabotage will be sufficient to get them to see the error of their ways. Shock tactics however, by their very nature, have a habit of tapering off and losing their potency. It may be necessary therefore to do more than this to sustain any initial gain. We need to look at the situation to see how to entice more from a coaster.

▶ Modify the situation

Coasters are circumstantial slackers. Their slacking is triggered either by an impending departure or the hope they will be offered early retirement or a redundancy package. Coasting is not therefore a behaviour which has always been characteristic. Indeed the opposite may well be the case: coasters could be hard workers who have decided to opt out. We need to consider ways to get them to opt back in again.

People who are leaving are an invaluable resource. Perhaps for the first time in their careers they feel liberated and able to 'tell it the way it is' with uninhibited honesty. They also have expertise which is about to be withdrawn and lost for ever. The answer is to work out how to extract the maximum advantage from the situation. Coasters could, for example, be required to prepare and give a presentation to top management, encapsulating the main lessons learned during their time with the organisation, together with recommendations for improvement. It would be the equivalent of a high-profile exit interview. Preparing for it would be a great motivator for the coaster and the organisation would stand to gain from listening to them.

Similarly, coasters could be given special projects or investigations to conduct that tapped into their expertise. One of the best ways to rejuvenate a coaster is to give them responsibility for coaching or mentoring less experienced people. This helps them overcome the feeling that it is futile to put themselves out and puts them on something of a pedestal as respected 'founts of wisdom'.

If all else fails you could have the equivalent of a swear box and fine the coaster every time he or she gloats or even mentions future plans!

Conservative

Conservative people are keen to preserve the status quo and there-fore resist changes. They tend to be backward-looking and to have feelings of nostalgia about the past. Everyone has 'comfort zones' beyond which they feel threatened and uncomfortable. Conservative people ring-fence themselves with smaller zones than radical people, who are happier to throw caution to the winds and experiment.

Conservative people are a problem in times of turbulence or change because they devote all their energy to maintaining the familiar and resisting the unfamiliar. Since there is nothing permanent except change, resistance is likely to be a frequent occurrence. This is especially true of transformational changes, the big ones where step-by-step modifications are inappropriate or inadequate. Incremental changes are less of a threat, but even they have a nasty habit of unexpectedly escalating into a transformational change.

THE OPTIONS

▶ **Do nothing**

Conservative people would be delighted if nothing happened. They could then stay happily within their comfort zones and carry on doing things exactly as they always have. This is clearly unsatisfactory if you are keen to make changes or to get the conservatives to make changes. If you are prepared to live with the status quo, do nothing; otherwise read on!

▶ **Alter your perception of the problem**

You could regard conservative people as useful safeguards against change for change's sake. They are hard to convince and that puts you on your mettle and compels you to have well-thought-out reasons for the change. So while it might be a bit far-fetched to suggest that resistors to change should be welcomed, they do perform a useful function in putting a brake on ill-considered changes.

This perception might help you to see how you could use conservative traditionalists as devil's advocates to force you to consider all the angles and implications before going ahead with a change.

▶ **Persuade the problem person to change**

Persuading a traditionalist to embrace change is worth trying but don't expect miracles. Conservative people have learned the hard way to be wary of changes. Perhaps an apparently innocent change in the past turned out to disadvantage them. Perhaps they remember how much they dislike the feelings of uncertainty and confusion that are inevitable in the early stages of any change. Such memories harden into attitudes and lie dormant, waiting to be activated at the first whiff of an impending change. Of course attitudes have been learned from experience and can therefore be updated by subsequent experiences. But conservative people are unfortunately extremely reluctant to admit that their attitudes have a limited life and could be amenable to modification. This is the very essence of conservatism: hang on to the old attitudes come what may!

Conservatives may intellectually concede the point that all changes can't be bad but none the less in practice succumb to traditionalist attitudes and dig in their heels. Reasoning and persuasion on their own are unlikely to do the job. A better bet is to combine persuasion with complementary modifications to the situation.

▶ Modify the situation

There are at least three ways to make change more palatable for resistant people.

First, you can lean over backwards to consult every inch of the way. A trigger for out-and-out resistance is a *fait accompli* announced out of the blue. Consultation, particularly early in the process, while options are fluid, softens the blow, and gives people some ownership of the change and a chance to get used to the idea.

Secondly, pace the changes and keep them as small as possible. Incremental changes introduced over a period of time are less threatening to conservatives and give them time to adjust gradually on a step-by-step basis.

Thirdly, if consultation is not feasible or the change is transformational and therefore does not lend itself to a phased introduction, you will have to use the 'force and support' approach. This is where you go ahead and impose the change regardless of opposition (of which there will be plenty), thus forcing conservatives to change their behaviour, and gamble that they will discover subsequently that it isn't so bad after all. A lot of legislation follows this pattern by forcing behaviour changes such as wearing seat belts, not discriminating and providing equal opportunities, in the hope that attitudes will eventually align themselves to the new behaviour. Obviously forcing people – especially conservatives – to change their behaviour is unlikely to be a popular tactic. You can make the process more palatable by actively supporting the new behaviours even though they have been imposed. Alas, this doesn't happen with legislation, where the emphasis is on punishing people who don't conform rather than rewarding those who do.

In practice a combination of persuasion to try and reduce resistance and 'force and support' is often necessary in the face of conservatism.

Defensive

Defensive people are brilliant at protecting themselves. They have a seemingly plausible explanation for everything. If they are late they can explain it, if they make a mistake they can explain it, if they break something they can explain it. This may spill over into buck-passing (see **Buck-passer**) or it may be a more subtle rationalisation of why they didn't succeed.

When things do not go according to plan they throw people into a state of dissonance. This is an unpleasant feeling caused by two conflicting ideas such as:

- it is essential to be punctual at all times
- on this occasion I am late

Dissonance is reduced by rationalising or downgrading our attachment to one of the conflicting ideas, for example:

- It is preferable but not absolutely essential to be punctual.
- I'm usually punctual but on this occasion I'm late because my cat died this morning, my car wouldn't start, the train was derailed, a volcano unexpectedly erupted . . .

Defensive behaviour *always* searches for explanations outside the person. The rationalising, or defence, mechanisms have usually been learned so thoroughly that they swing into play virtually automatically as a means of achieving consonance.

The problem with defensiveness is that it prevents people from accepting responsibility for their own actions and creates a formidable barrier to learning from experience. Defensive people tend to repeat the same mistakes and having done so repeat the same explanations!

THE OPTIONS

▶ **Do nothing**

Quite often defensive explanations are relatively harmless. They protect the person and help them to feel happier. At other times they blind people to the folly of their own actions and inhibit the vital process of continuous improvement. If you do nothing you are thereby condoning the cosy practice of rationalising and the tendency to see the world through rose-coloured spectacles.

▶ **Alter your perception of the problem**

You could persuade yourself that defensive people have missed their true vocation – as politicians naturally! You could play to their strengths and give them subordinates who need a protectionist boss. Other than this it is difficult to see any advantage in altering your perception. Indeed to do so might amount to an attempt on your part to rationalise the problem away!

▶ **Persuade the problem person to change**

The best tactic is to confront the defensive person and to allow them to go on the defensive about their defensiveness. Choose a time when they have slipped up and made a mistake of some kind and invite them to join you in analysing why the mistake occurred and what should be done in future to avoid its repetition. Naturally they will proffer an explanation. Don't resist it; accept it and ask, 'So what are you going to do differently in future?' The 'you' in this question is deliberate. It puts the monkey firmly back on their shoulder and forces them to take responsibility.

Predictably this will provoke more defensiveness. If you repeat the formula, again and again if need be, the defensive person will eventually capitulate and accept responsibility for their part in the mistake. Persistent challenges are the best way to break through the defensive barriers with which such people surround themselves.

▶ Modify the situation

No one was born defensive: they learned to be in order to protect themselves from accusations of wrong-doing from parents and teachers. What matters now, however, is not an examination of how defensive behaviours came into being but an understanding of what it is in the current situation that sustains the habit. Possible triggers for defensiveness are when:

- they are under attack or being criticised
- something has gone wrong or not as well as required.

Possible payoffs for defensive behaviour are that:

- the attack is repelled
- the attacker apologises
- the need to change things is avoided.

The triggers can be modified by, for example, taking the wind out of the defensive person's sails and accepting some responsibility yourself. This may strike you as inappropriately ingratiating, but a softly-softly approach is essential to stop the defensive barriers' being raised. So start by asking for their advice, initially about what *you* should do differently, and then slowly turn it round to establish what *they* are going to do differently. This becomes a 'we' approach rather than risking an accusational 'you' approach.

The payoffs clearly point to the folly of being fobbed off with defensive explanations. The more the person is defensive, the more determined you should be not to let them off the hook. By contrast, when they accept responsibility you should ease up on them. In this way they will learn that defensiveness doesn't pay, and it will gradually diminish.

Ditherer

People who dither are hesitant and indecisive. They are reluctant to close down options and make a decision one way or the other. They agonise over the merits of different options because they can see pros and cons of each, which naturally cancel each other out.

Indecisive people are a problem because their dithering delays decisions which need to be taken faster. Some decisions can wait (though it doesn't necessarily follow that the longer it takes to reach a decision the better it will be), and others have to be taken quickly or the moment is past. Ditherers miss opportunities and exasperate people who look to them to be more decisive.

THE OPTIONS

▶ **Do nothing**

The more you pressurise a ditherer the more their misgivings increase and the likelihood of a quick decision decreases. On the other hand if you do nothing, indecisive people will continue to dither. The chances are that they won't even see it as dithering. They will convince themselves that there is merit in taking time over a decision and be critical of 'gung ho' people (see **Impulsive**) who shoot from the hip and ask questions afterwards. Ditherers will also rationalise that delays often allow new information to come to light which can cast a new light on a decision. The irony is that the more you put pressure on a ditherer the more determined (i.e. decisive) he or she will be *not* to be pitchforked into a decision!

▶ **Alter your perception of the problem**

You could see ditherers as being admirably circumspect, determined to think through the consequences before making their minds up. They have learned, perhaps from bitter experience, that hasty decisions taken in the heat of the moment are invariably bad ones which are later regretted or have to be reversed. Dogmatic people (see **Dogmatic**) are incisive and make decisions quickly because they tend to jump to conclusions regardless of the facts. Subsequently they have to become even more dogmatic as they staunchly defend the correctness of their decisions in the face of criticism (or make a U-turn while maintaining that they are doing no such thing). Ditherers avoid this trap by investing effort *before* an irrevocable decision is made.

This perception may help you to be more patient with ditherers and to be more diligent in furnishing them with good-quality information upon which they can rely to reach decisions that even they consider to be the soundest that could have been made 'all things considered' (a suitable epitaph for a ditherer).

▶ Persuade the problem person to change

Ditherers need to be persuaded that there is no such thing as the 'right' decision, only the best one in the circumstances. No decision is ever taken with every scrap of pertinent information available. Waiting allows more information to become available, but this provides no comfort since you never know how much more would be revealed if you waited just that little bit longer. Logically, ditherers would therefore wait for ever.

Ditherers are reassured if they at least have adequate arguments marshalled to defend the efficacy of their decisions should they be challenged. Counsel them to concentrate their attentions on having a convincing case rather than on leaving no stone unturned in their bid to make perfect decisions. This eases some of the self-imposed pressure by focusing on how to sell their decisions and fretting less about whether they are good enough. Who knows, the indecisive person may even discover the merits of empowering others to make decisions – and letting them do their own dithering!

▶ Modify the situation

Ditherers are more inclined to be indecisive when wrestling with open-ended problems where there are many equally viable options. Problems with one demonstrably correct answer are less threatening. The worst nightmare for a ditherer is to have to choose between a variety of options with the pros and cons of each finely balanced.

The answer is to reduce the choices or to make the open-ended problems appear more like single-answer ones. This can be achieved by presenting ditherers with thought-through cases, listing all the pros and cons but getting them to come down clearly in favour of one well-argued recommendation.

Another approach is to list the criteria that form the basis of a decision and invite the ditherer to put them in priority order and give a weighting to each. A preferred decision then emerges once the weighted criteria are applied. This apparently objective way of dealing with subjective judgements and fine discriminations takes the uncertainty out of decision making and makes it seem more rational and 'scientific'.

Time limits are another variable to play with. The more pressing a decision the more ditherers are compelled to come off the fence. They won't like it one bit but necessity works wonders.

After a ditherer has made a decision, it is predictable that they will suffer pangs of doubt and that these will be particularly strong if they have been hustled into making a quick decision. It is vital, therefore, to help the indecisive person achieve consonance by using every reasonable opportunity to reinforce the correctness of their decision. The less they have dithered the more the decision should be supported; the more they have dithered the less the decision should be supported. This isn't always possible, of course, but it isn't a bad tactic with the indecisive.

Dogmatic

Dogmatic people tend to be opinionated and rigid. They are the sort of people who make 'iffy' things sound cut and dried. You will never find a dogmatic person saying, 'On the one hand this . . . but on the other hand that.' They cannot bring themselves to be so even-handed. Dogmatic people have one point of view (theirs) and stick to it. They therefore come across as intransigent and uncompromising.

Obstinate, dogmatic people can be a problem because they are difficult to influence. They tend to jump to a conclusion and that's that. If you happen to share the same conclusion, fine; but if you hold a different point of view you will need all your persuasive skills to make any impact. Dogmatic people are impervious to logical arguments ('Don't bother me with the facts') and quickly take up a position and refuse to budge.

THE OPTIONS

▶ **Do nothing**

If you can live with dogma, or perhaps even find it convenient because it saves you having to reach your own conclusions, then do nothing. If, on the other hand (a dogmatic person would not accept there was an 'other hand'!), the dogma is getting in your way, then you'd best do something, even if it only amounts to damage limitation.

▶ **Alter your perception of the problem**

You could perceive the dogmatic person as principled and resolute. In these uncertain times, it could be useful to have someone who is unswerving. Stubbornness can be a tower of strength, a rallying point and an inspiration to the faint-hearted.

This perception could help you to see that, provided the person is being dogmatic about things you agree with (a vital proviso), you haven't got a problem. You have someone who isn't afraid to say what they think and who can be trusted to stick to the party line through thick and thin. A dogmatic person makes a splendid ally. Problems only arise when they take up a position which differs markedly from your own.

▶ **Persuade the problem person to change**

Dogmatic people are notoriously difficult to persuade. They make their minds up quickly and throw all their energies into proving that they are right. The more you attempt to get them to change their mind, the more they dig their heels in and refuse to budge. This stubborn streak will inevitably extend to the subject of their dogmatism. If you dare raise the subject, they are bound to take it as a challenge and set to work to convince you that they are right and you are wrong.

An oblique approach is best so that they are not compelled to take up a position and defend it to the hilt. Don't let them back themselves into a corner. So don't accuse them of being dogmatic; don't use the word at all. Instead make it clear that you welcome their opinions and would find it more helpful to have not just the conclusion they have reached, but also the 'pros and cons'. Explain how their persuasiveness will be enhanced if they offer both sides of the argument so that the rationale for their opinion is open to inspection. Show them how their conclusions are *faits accomplis* to everyone else and that this increases incomprehension and resistance.

Demonstrate the impressiveness of the 'pros and cons' approach by offering some yourself in this connection. For example, the advantages of giving some pros and cons with an opinion are that:

- it shows how the opinion or conclusion has been reached
- it avoids the appearance of one-sidedness
- it shows respect for the other person as a mature, thinking person
- it makes it likely that the pros and cons will be the focus of attention and avoids an unhelpful slanging match over the opinion itself.

The disadvantages are that:

- the cons may outweigh the pros
- the other person might get into a muddle and prefer to 'have it straight'.

Stop here and invite them to think of some more advantages.

If this approach works you will have succeeded in persuading the dogmatic person to do something they would never normally do. It is likely that their thought processes will still be the wrong way round, jumping to a conclusion first and identifying the pros and cons afterwards, but openly offering some advantages and disadvantages is a singularly undogmatic thing to do.

▶ Modify the situation

Dogmatic people are more likely to jump to conclusions and hold on to them stubbornly in certain situations. At other times they will be less dogmatic. Possible triggers for dogmatism could be when:

- a topic touches on strongly held beliefs or conclusions previously reached
- other people appear to be dithering and indecisive
- the person's opinion is attacked or challenged
- ambiguity is high, for example when dealing with open-ended problems with no 'right' answer.

These triggers help us to appreciate that uncertainty is like a red rag to a bull for a dogmatic person. Their tolerance of ambiguity is particularly low and in these circumstances they experience a strong compulsion to latch on to a conclusion. The security of the conclusion means that if challenged, they will defend it fiercely and rapidly become intransigent. The more clear-cut the situation the more relaxed dogmatic people are likely to be. What's more, where there is likely to be a correct way of doing things, dogma may be more appropriate. Unhelpful dogma will therefore be reduced if dogmatic people are able to stay within their 'comfort zones' i.e. in relatively structured situations where uncertainty is minimised. Dogmatic people are at their best after a decision has been made and second thoughts are unwelcome.

Possible payoffs for dogmatic behaviour could be that:

- there is an increase in certainty and reduction in ambiguity
- people stop arguing and apparently agree with the dogmatic person
- people show their appreciation for 'strong' leadership and decisiveness.

It is important not to deprive the dogmatic person of these payoffs, otherwise they will be unnerved and retreat into increased dogma. The less they are dogmatic the more they should be 'rewarded' with agreement and the more dogmatic they are the more it should be countered with opposition. This is a reversal of the usual state of affairs.

Eccentric

Eccentrics are people who 'do their own thing' and do not conform to commonly accepted conventions. Their behaviour is deemed to be odd because they deviate from whatever everyone else considers to be 'normal'.

Whether eccentric behaviour is a problem or not largely depends on how people react. Sometimes the eccentricity is regarded with amusement while at other times it causes offence. For example, if someone wore carpet slippers in the office it would probably attract attention and a few sniggers. If, however, they wore their carpet slippers to a formal meeting it would be more likely to be regarded as offensive, even if the eccentric's behaviour at the meeting was in other respects 'normal'.

THE OPTIONS

▶ Do nothing

Eccentrics are often seeking attention so, if you want to deprive them of their payoff, ignore the behaviour. It is unlikely that this will be sufficient to cure the eccentric, partly because other people's reactions may be reinforcing the behaviour and partly because eccentrics are often pig-headed enough to carry on 'doing their own thing' regardless. If the eccentricity is harmless and amusing, leave well alone and do nothing.

▶ Alter your perception of the problem

You could see eccentrics as a real asset. They are courageous people who risk challenging conventionality and conservatism. This helps us to be less pompous and unquestioningly accepting. It rarely means that we will emulate the eccentricity but at least it helps us to be more conscious of conventions that we adopt unthinkingly. If you find it difficult to see how eccentric behaviour can perform a useful function, you can at least perceive eccentrics as entertainers bringing added interest and amusement into our lives.

▶ Persuade the problem person to change

If you are confident that the eccentric behaviour really matters, then you must take action to curtail it. If, for example, a sale was lost because a prospective client took a dim view of carpet slippers being worn in a meeting, then carpet slippers in meetings with outsiders must be banned. This does not mean that the wearing of carpet slippers in all situations at work must cease; only when doing so has a detrimental effect on the organisation. In this way eccentric behaviour is confined but not eradicated.

Usually a quiet word will suffice. Eccentrics are often thick-skinned and cannot believe that their behaviour might cause offence. Giving them feedback and drawing attention to the fact that the customer took umbrage should be sufficient. You are unlikely to dent the eccentric's basic beliefs about freedom of expression but then you don't need to do that in order to stop them being eccentric on particular occasions.

▶ Modify the situation

Eccentrics are eccentric because it suits them and blow everybody else. If a quiet word will suffice then there is no need to bring about a change by modifying the situation. If, however, the eccentricity persists in situations where it causes real offence and is troublesome then you need to look to the circumstances themselves. Either the eccentric and the people who are likely to take umbrage must be kept apart or, if this isn't feasible, advance warning should be given to reduce the impact. Odd behaviour isn't so odd if you are expecting it, and so an explanation is a sensible exercise in damage limitation.

Flippant

Flippant people make light of things which in your opinion should be taken more seriously. When to be earnest and when to be frivolous is always a matter of judgement. Flippant people get it wrong and so cause offence. They can also be a problem because they distract attention from the matter in hand. For example, if you are trying to tackle a serious problem by exploring all the options before taking action, the last thing you want is someone making wisecracks. Misplaced levity is particularly offensive to people with a puritanical streak and those who have a Calvinistic work ethic.

THE OPTIONS

▶ **Do nothing**

If the flippancy is intermittent rather than incessant and does not cause undue offence then this is an option worth considering. Sometimes flippant remarks serve a useful function. They can ease tension and give people a well-earned breather between bouts of intense concentration. If, however, the flippancy is excessive and causing annoyance then it is best to tackle the problem rather than let it pass unchecked.

▶ **Alter your perception of the problem**

Flippancy is very much in the eye of the beholder. It may well be that what you regard as unacceptable flippancy someone else regards as a bit of harmless fun. Perhaps you should ask yourself why you are so easily offended and set about raising your tolerance level. You could regard the flippant person as performing a useful function rather akin to a court jester. Seeing the funny side of things helps to keep a more balanced perspective. Flippant remarks may spark ideas in other people that they would not otherwise have had or dared to voice. In this sense, flippant remarks could act as a catalyst in rather the same way that wild ideas do during a brainstorming session.

▶ **Persuade the problem person to change**

It isn't too difficult to show a flippant person the error of their ways. Flippancy is really an error of judgement, a failure to distinguish between appropriate humour and frivolity. Moreover, the chances are that if a flippant person reduced the frequency of their remarks they would no longer cause offence or even be regarded as flippant.

Sit down with the person and draw up a list of situations where flippant remarks are banned. The list should feature occasions where you want people to take the topic seriously, for example when planning a restructuring where some redundancies are inevitable, or when disciplining a poor performer. The list should also include encounters with certain people who have a low tolerance for levity.

A second list should identify situations where a certain amount of light-heartedness is not a problem. In these cases wisecracks should be 'rationed' to no more than two or three per hour.

Flippancy is not banned or rationed in situations that don't appear on either list but the agreement is to review the plan constantly and add items to the list in the light of experience. The idea of legislating for something spontaneous like flippancy may seem a little odd. The whole idea however is to reduce the flippant person's discretion and to help them see that there is a time and place for spontaneity and a time and place for behaviour to be consciously controlled.

▶ Modify the situation

It is likely that people you regard as flippant take some situations seriously. If you could identify the circumstances that provide frivolity and contrast them with the situations where their humour is acceptable you would have the key to modifying the situation.

Possible triggers for flippancy might be when:

- the person is 'coasting' or a bystander to the main events
- the person is feeling bored and mischievous
- a kindred spirit is present, i.e. someone else who tends to flippancy
- everyone else is being unduly earnest or serious.

The best hope is to keep the person busy so that they are not tempted to be mischievous as an antidote to boredom. Give them the chair, or the minutes to take, or a flip chart to write on – any role that keeps them involved in the mainstream of events.

Flippant people indulge in this behaviour because they enjoy it and are convinced it is harmless. Possible payoffs for them are that:

- people laugh
- they feel less bored
- 'over-serious' people become indignant
- it's fun (particularly if there are other flippant people to spark off).

Flippant people's payoffs are primarily to do with the reactions of other people. If flippant remarks were ignored it is predictably that, after a while, they would decrease. Unfortunately signing everyone up to ignore flippancy is unlikely to be a practical option. It might be more feasible to rebuke the problem person immediately after each flippant remark. This runs the risk of drawing undue attention to the flippancy, attention which the person might for a time relish. But if you persisted and then, when the frequency of flippant remarks started to drop, steadfastly ignored them, flippancy would no longer be advantageous.

The most promising recipe for flippancy is a combination of the rationing system described earlier and being painstaking in not letting unwarranted flippancy pass without a rebuke. Inevitably, the flippant person will think you a real pain in the neck and you must judge whether that is a price worth paying.

Gamesman

The word 'gamesmanship' was coined by Stephen Potter. His definition of it is 'the art of winning games by talk or behaviour designed to put off one's opponent'. The well-known book by Eric Berne, *Games People Play*, added a further 'psychological' dimension to games. He maintained that games are unhealthy transactions between people where there is a hidden agenda for one person to 'win' at another's expense. A crucial difference is that gamesmanship is conscious and calculated, whereas psychological games are unconscious. Berne gave many examples of games: 'Yes but', 'Harried', 'Lunch bag', 'Now I've got you . . .', 'Uproar', 'Poor me'. In each case there is a win-lose outcome.

Games are a problem because they absorb time and energy and finish up with the 'victim' feeling put down or inadequate. In the 'Yes but' game, for example, help with a problem is ostensibly invited but when ideas are proffered they are met with, 'Yes but . . .' rejections. The helper has unwittingly walked into a trap where the ulterior motive is to prove the inadequacy of anything that might be suggested. Without realising it the helper is on a hiding to nothing from the start. The game finishes with the would-be helper feeling bad and the 'yes but-er' feeling good because he or she had demonstrated that their problem was so special that it could not be solved. In a subsequent interaction the tables are likely to be turned when the victim ensnares the other person in one of their games.

THE OPTIONS

▶ **Do nothing**

Games are rife in most work places. If you do nothing, it is guaranteed that they will continue and people will get hurt. An exception is when you have lost out as a result of someone else's game. If you manage to resist the urge to get your own back and instead opt to do nothing, you would at least have done your bit to break the repetitive cycle. This however assumes that you can identify games, albeit with the benefit of hindsight, and have sufficient self-awareness to prevent yourself from being a player.

▶ **Alter your perception of the problem**

The realisation that so many games happen outside the awareness of the players is at the same time helpful and unhelpful. It is helpful because it gives the players the benefit of the doubt; they aren't *deliberately* scheming to win at other people's expense. It is unhelpful because unconscious goings-on are usually harder to detect and do something about.

The perception that psychological games are innocent at a conscious level, coupled with the realisation that it takes two to play, could help you to be more tolerant and understanding. You might study your own predilection for certain games and see if you can nip them in the bud, before turning your attention on games other people play. At the very least you could practise choosing not to take on the bad feelings after a game which you lost.

▶ **Persuade the problem person to change**

Games are intriguing and it isn't difficult to interest people in them. The best approach with a game player is to start by focusing on games other people play and let it slowly dawn that no one is exempt. Encourage your game player to read a classic like *I'm OK – You're OK* by Tom Harris and to become aware of the games they initiate and get sucked into. Be careful, however, not to start condoning another game called 'Spot the game'!

▶ Modify the situation

All games, whether conscious or unconscious, are played in anticipation of a win at someone else's expense. This is a strong pay-off and ensures that games become repetitive, well-established behaviour patterns.

The most obvious way to change the situation is to refuse to play. In practice this isn't quite as straightforward as it seems because games are difficult to detect at the time they are happening. In the game of 'Yes but', for example, it is only after you have suffered a few rebuttals that you begin to suspect that things may not be all that they seem. As soon as this dawns on you the answer is to come clean about your suspicions by saying something like 'You asked for my help and yet every time I suggest an idea you reject it. I feel as if I'm on a hiding to nothing and I've better things to do.' If you adopt this hard line do not relent when, predictably, the game player protests their innocence. You must walk away to deprive them of their payoff.

With practice you will become better at spotting games early on and even start to anticipate games that are typical of certain people before they start. It is essential to guard against smugness, however, otherwise you may find you have unwittingly become embroiled in another game.

Gossip

Gossips spend unproductive time talking about people behind their backs. It is usually inconsequential but it can become malicious and harmful to people's reputations. Gossips are often given to exaggeration in a bid to spice things up a bit and intrigue their listeners. This is often the process that feeds the grapevine and gives birth to rumours. Gossiping can be a problem for two reasons. First, it can be time-consuming. People frequently gossip when they should be doing something more productive. Secondly, when gossip is malicious it undermines people's credibility and can lead to scaremongering, uncertainty and low morale. Rumours have a nasty habit of becoming self-fulfilling prophecies.

THE OPTIONS

▶ **Do nothing**

It is easy to turn a blind eye to gossiping. You can rationalise that people need to have a good natter occasionally and convince yourself that once the gossiping is over people settle down and are more productive, not less. Any decision to intervene clearly depends on the extent and nature of the gossiping. If gossips frequently succeed in distracting you or other people from work, or what they say is malicious, then doing nothing will in effect condone it.

▶ **Alter your perception of the problem**

You could see gossips as an important channel of communication. Feed them titbits of information and let them do the rest. This could be particularly useful with bad news, when you may want people to fear the worst so that, when the news eventually breaks, it isn't as bad as the rumours had led them to believe. The gossip's tendency to exaggerate and embellish could work to your advantage. By contrast, it would be important to keep good news away from the gossips lest their powers of exaggeration push up expectations to the extent that when the news is released it comes as an anti-climax.

▶ **Persuade the problem person to change**

Gossipers consider gossiping to be a harmless activity and will therefore need to be convinced that it is something they should curtail. The unproductive time it consumes is probably the most promising angle to take. It would be harder to prove the extent to which it had been malicious. Collect some facts by keeping a diary for a week or so where you log the time taken in idle gossip. You could also note how many people were involved or distracted by the gossiping. Then calculate the total man-hours spent gossiping and, if you want to be really sophisticated and have information about salaries, work out a cost per five minutes' worth of gossip.

These preparations are worth the effort in order to prove that gossiping is not as innocent and harmless as gossips believe. Choose a moment to feed this information to them and suggest that gossiping is confined to official breaks. Don't expect to solve the problem so simply. You will need more than one shot at it, with a quiet reminder that 'gossiping costs money' each time it occurs.

▶ Modify the situation

People gossip because the situation permits them to. Gossiping is a discretionary activity, to which they rapidly become 'addicted'. Somehow the mould needs to be broken. This can be done in at least three ways.

First, if the gossips were physically separated they couldn't gossip. It might be worth rearranging the office to keep the arch-gossips apart. At the very least this will inconvenience them and make it more difficult to congregate.

Secondly, you could work out how to reduce the gossips' discretion, preferably by giving them more work and keeping them busy.

Thirdly, consider how to engineer events so that gossiping is confined to a particular place and time. Breaks are obviously ideal. If people were allocated an official gossiping slot the chances are that it would seem so absurd, and the gossips would feel so self-conscious, that it would kill it off. Even if it didn't, confining gossip to the times when it is least disruptive is clearly desirable. You could designate a special place and put up a big notice saying 'Gossiping Area'!

Humourless

Humourless people tend to be too intense, serious and earnest for your taste. It's in the eye of the beholder of course, but when people don't laugh at your jokes, don't join in light-hearted banter and generally take themselves too seriously, you are likely to find them hard going. It is always easier to interact with kindred spirits who share your sense of humour than with people who aren't on your wavelength.

Strictly speaking there are probably no really humourless people, only people who have a different sense of humour from your own. Senses of humour vary from the loud and 'whacky' to the subtle and dry. If you are at the loud end of the scale you might miss the subtleties of the dry quip delivered with a straight face. Certainly people without a 'Goon Show' or 'Monty Python' sense of humour are likely to be poor creative thinkers. They will find it difficult to indulge in something as 'silly' as lateral thinking where the essence is suddenly seeing connections between things that were previously unrelated. There are strong associations between right-brained, creative thinking and humour. People who, in your judgement, take things too seriously are probably more inclined to be left-brained and analytical.

THE OPTIONS

▶ Do nothing

The chances are that your humourless person is a bit of a drag and not much fun to be with, but that being earnest doesn't have a detrimental effect on their performance. If this is the case, it is undoubtedly wiser to leave well alone and not make an issue of it. If, however, their seriousness hampers them in the performance of their work, then you'll need to do something. They might, for example, be hampered when breaking the ice with people and establishing rapport. It might be important that they free-up and think more laterally. They may often be in tricky situations where it would help to use humour to ease tensions or defuse strong emotions. Perhaps they are in a role where they have to give the occasional light-hearted speech. All these are examples of situations in which doing something will help to enhance the person's job performance rather than just making them a more amusing companion.

▶ Alter your perception of the problem

Instead of branding the person as humourless you could assume that they have a sense of humour but that it eludes you. It could be quite fun tracking it down and learning to appreciate it. You might discover alternative senses of humour to add to your repertoire. The crucial change in perception is the insistence that everyone has a sense of humour even if it may not be immediately apparent.

Alternatively, if you insist that they are humourless you could come to perceive them as a useful counterbalance to your own tendency to take things too light-heartedly. Their seriousness could be a helpful steadying influence preventing you from escalating into over-the-top mania. Perhaps the strengths of your creative right brain need to be complemented by the strengths of their analytical left brain. The dovetailing of differences between people often results in a winning combination. After all, the success of many famous comics has depended on someone playing the straight-man. Perhaps you too could use the equivalent of a straight-man?

▶ Persuade the problem person to change

There is no point in accusing someone of not having a sense of humour. They are bound to deny it and would be right to do so. It would be the equivalent of telling someone they haven't got any taste when what you really mean is that their tastes differ from your own.

If you want to modify your apparently humourless person it would be more productive to focus on one or two of the behaviours they manifest that are detrimental to their performance. It could be their difficulty in establishing rapport, for example, or their reluctance to join whole-heartedly in a brainstorming session. By concentrating on manifest behaviours you never need mention anything about a vague indefinable thing such as a sense of humour.

When you have decided what behaviours to focus on you could sit down with the problem person and work out a realistic action plan. Depending on the behaviours you have chosen, there are plenty of well-tried techniques that could usefully come to the rescue. Techniques to foster right-brained thinking abound. Brainstorming is but one example. People can also be helped to remember and tell jokes of the shaggy-dog variety or, better still, to adapt some standard jokes so that they make them custom-built. The safest jokes are always ones told against yourself, so you could help your problem person concoct some jokes about not having a sense of humour!

▶ Modify the situation

People's sense of humour is likely to wax and wane depending on circumstances. In this punitive world plenty of things happen to people that they don't find in the least funny, from being stuck in an inconvenient traffic jam to being made redundant to learning that you have a life-threatening disease or that someone near and dear to you has died. So, as always, circumstances play a significant part.

It is likely that in certain situations your problem person will be serious and in others they will be relatively jovial. The word 'relatively' is important here because even when they are jovial, they may seem earnest by your standards. Triggers for an apparent lack of humour may be when:

- everyone else is being flippant

- there is a problem to be solved
- something unpleasant has happened to the person
- the person is feeling out of their depth, anxious or unable to cope.

Possible payoffs for being serious are that:

- people calm down and take things more seriously
- sensible solutions to problems are generated
- people sympathise.

Creative thinking techniques offer a clue about how to design a situation so that it forces the required behaviours. Paradoxically the answer seems to be to structure the situation and not to rely on people being in the right mood or on something as fickle as spontaneity. So serious people are more likely to see the funny side of things if they are in a situation where it is temporarily OK to let their hair down. It must be temporary, otherwise their serious side will start to ask questions about inappropriate frivolity. Brainstorming, for example, can only be kept up for short periods of between ten and 20 minutes. Humour similarly comes and goes in short bursts. People who are inclined to be serious need to be put into situations that give them 'permission' to loosen up so that they can discover that humour is the shortest distance between two people and that if anything it enhances the quality of solutions to problems rather than detracting from them.

Impulsive

Impulsive people can be a joy or a menace. They are a joy when spontaneity is appropriate but a menace when it is necessary to play it by the book. Impulsive people are often carried away by their own enthusiasm and, of course, they see their behaviour as an asset rather than a problem.

Impulsive people create problems when you want consistency. They are inclined to be unpredictable and arbitrary, depending on the mood they are in. They have scant regard for anything bureaucratic (see **Bureaucrat**), for rules, regulations and procedures. Their philosophy is very much that 'rules are there to be broken'. There are plenty of occasions when this is admirable but unfortunately impulsive people are not very good at judging when to switch their impulsiveness on and off. They are therefore inclined to behave impulsively when it is singularly inappropriate and this often has far-reaching and damaging consequences. For example, many employment practices to do with hiring, firing and safety at work are regulated by legislation. Left to their own devices impulsive managers would ride roughshod through such restrictive red tape and hire and fire on a whim.

Such discretionary behaviour is frowned upon because it is the enemy of order, standardisation and quality. All legislation, whether in society at large or within an organisation or community, is an attempt to curtail impulsive behaviour. Not to do so would result in anarchy and chaos.

THE OPTIONS

▶ Do nothing

Doing nothing about appropriate impulsiveness is fine. It promotes individual flair and creativity and is infinitely preferable to the drab 'sameness' of over-regulation. Doing nothing about inappropriate impulsiveness is not recommended, no matter how much 'prima donnas' might protest about their style being cramped.

The trick, therefore, is to distinguish between situations where impulsiveness is positive and helpful and where it is negative and unhelpful. Usually impulsive behaviour is fine in short concentrated bursts and within clear parameters. It is not acceptable in situations where consistency is essential. Thus predictable, regulated behaviour is necessary when driving on roads with speed limits, traffic lights, pedestrian crossings and the like. Impulsive driving is fine on race tracks designed for the purpose with no on-coming traffic or pedestrians and with safety barriers.

▶ Alter your perception of the problem

The obvious shift in perception is to regard impulsive people as creative innovators, a welcome source of inspiration to deferential bureaucrats. In rather the same way that right-brained lateral thinkers are essential during brainstorming sessions and left-brained analytical thinkers are essential afterwards to sort out the wheat from the chaff, so impulsive people are essential to offset bureaucratic people. It isn't an either/or choice. They are complementary and both are necessary at different stages in the process.

If, therefore, you saw impulsive people as invaluable innovators, counterbalancing the unimaginative and pedestrian, you would be in a better frame of mind to use them appropriately and curse them less.

▶ Persuade the problem person to change

Impulsive people can be persuaded to curtail their enthusiasm for bending the rules, but it is essential not to overdo it and thus destroy a behaviour which is an asset in certain situations. The best approach is to sit down with them and brainstorm some guidelines on when to be impulsive and when not to be. For example, impulsive behaviour might be appropriate when:

- the likelihood of creating awkward precedents is low
- people are not likely to be upset about inequitable treatment
- it is relatively safe to experiment
- the person is dealing with small numbers of people who all know each other
- you are brainstorming ideas
- people need to be inspired.

Impulsive behaviour is inappropriate when:

- you are implementing something on an across-the-board basis
- it is vital to get it right, as when safety is at a premium or it could create awkward precedents for example
- large numbers of people are involved
- the pros and cons of a particular course of action are being analysed
- policy is being made
- you are saying something on the record that will be referred to and could be quoted back to you.

These are only generic examples. More pertinent guidelines should result from a session where you focus on typical situations that arise at work. Once agreed guidelines exist, it is easier to give feedback to the person and to add to the guidelines as and when new situations arise.

▶ Modify the situation

Even the most impulsive person is cautious in certain situations. If you believe that their impulsiveness is situational rather than exclusively temperamental, then you need to identify the ingredients in your situation that are associated with impulsiveness. Possible triggers might be when:

- rebelling against 'petty' rules and 'unnecessary' bureaucracy
- speaking extempore
- reacting emotionally in the heat of the moment.

Possible payoffs for impulsiveness might be:

- people's reactions – approval and admiration from kindred spirits, shock and horror from bureaucrats
- getting away with it on a significant number of occasions
- getting a 'buzz' from the freedom and creativity of making things up 'on the hoof'
- keeping people 'on their toes' by constantly chopping and changing and being inconsistent.

As we have already seen, impulsiveness is not a behaviour we want to eliminate completely. It has its time and place. Triggers and payoffs help us to see that there are likely to be many situational factors that maintain the tendency. Each trigger contains something that could be modified to reduce impulsiveness and increase circumspection. For example, pettiness could be reduced and preparation could be increased. Ways need to be found to build preparation into the system otherwise it is something that impulsive people will always skimp. So far as payoffs are concerned, the answer is to find ways to reverse some of the existing payoffs after the person has been inappropriately impulsive. If they got away with it less often and, by contrast, were rewarded for being circumspect more often then the balance would change. It is unlikely that this would bring about an overnight transformation but that is par for the course when modifying entrenched behaviour patterns.

Intimidator

Intimidators delight in throwing their weight around with people weaker than themselves. The intimidation can take many forms. It might involve:

- victimisation or bullying (by being unduly harsh and punitive)
- brow-beating and harassing (by nagging and chasing)
- domineering (by not listening, name-dropping, pulling rank and talking down to people).

Whatever form the intimidation takes, it is always focused on particular people. A boss, for example, may victimise some of his or her subordinates while being lenient and charming to others. A salesperson may harass some of his or her customers while soft-pedalling with others. A chauvinist may talk down to women (or more probably *some* women) but be deferential towards men. It is as though the intimidator has a way of dividing people into two categories: those that are susceptible to bullying and those that are not.

Intimidating behaviour is a problem because, when it works, victims become immobilised by fear. They live in a constant state of anxiety about making mistakes which makes them ultra-cautious and, ironically more accident-prone. They become subservient and submissive in a vain attempt to placate the intimidator. People who in different circumstances would sparkle and take the initiative become timid, downtrodden and depressed. If you doubt their ability to be more buoyant, watch how they behave when the intimidator is absent. Punitive regimes have to work hard to maintain control and, at best, they only manage to suppress initiative temporarily. As soon as there is a relaxation, human ingenuity reasserts itself with renewed vigour. While all is not lost in the long run, it doesn't seem like it in the short term if you are a victim.

THE OPTIONS

▶ Do nothing

This is exactly what the intimidator is hoping you will do. Bullies derive enormous satisfaction from submissive reactions. It is proof to them that bullying works. So you must certainly do something.

▶ Alter your perception of the problem

Admittedly this will be difficult if you are suffering at the hands of an intimidator, but you could come to see that, in a sense, it is your fault. You are being victimised because you let yourself be. Of course, this may strike you as an outrageous claim but if it takes two to argue, it takes two to intimidate. Somehow the way you react must be sufficiently encouraging to the intimidator for them to try it again and again until it settles into a consistent pattern.

This perception may help you see that your own behaviour holds the key to bringing about an improvement.

▶ Persuade the problem person to change

If you feel intimidated you are unlikely to be in a fit state to grasp the nettle and confront the bully. It would be extraordinarily courageous of you to do so – a David versus Goliath situation (although the good news is that David won!). You might find it more feasible to modify the situation rather than tackle the intimidator head on. However, if you *could* pluck up the courage and raise the topic, you would undoubtedly score brownie points with the intimidator. Bullies tend to be secretly impressed with people who stand up to them. It won't show at the time and they will never admit it, but the intimidator's respect for you will grow and, if you keep plugging away (see below) the intimidation is likely to decrease.

▶ Modify the situation

If we assume that the intimidator is picking on you because you are a 'push-over' then the key to changing the situation lies in your own behaviour. There will be things you inadvertently do to invite the bullying and reactions that encourage its repetition.

The toughest part is to discover what it is about your behaviour that triggers the intimidation. Ask yourself when it happens (not why; *when* is a more useful question that avoids speculation about the intimidator's motives), and analyse the different occasions to see if there are some common denominators. Does it happen:

- in the morning or in the afternoon?
- in a particular place?
- in public or in private?
- when you have said or done something?
- when something has happened to put pressure on the intimidator?

The answers to 'when' questions such as these will help you to be clearer about the triggers. Each trigger offers a potential clue to how you might modify the situation. If for example, you discover that intimidation occurs when you sit demurely behind your desk avoiding eye contact with the intimidator, then you could try standing and looking him or her in the eye. If you find you are picked on in public, say in an open-plan office or in a particular meeting, you could try moving your desk to a different position and sitting alongside the intimidator in meetings. The recipe will differ depending on your analysis of the situation. Even small modifications that you might reject as trivial are worth a try. Research shows that victims of street muggings walk less confidently and purposefully than people who don't get mugged. This is a good example of how little things can have a significant effect on the situation.

Even if you draw a blank with the triggers, either because your analysis doesn't reveal any common denominators or because you decide you are powerless to make any changes, all is not lost; an analysis of your reactions when you are intimidated may prove more fruitful. The chances are that your intimidator bullies you repeatedly because you react in a way which gives them some satisfaction. You might be doing this in a whole host of ways that amount to being submissive. If you react by being unduly apologetic or become silent and fail to express your point of view or feelings altogether, you are reacting in a way that allows the bully to be aggressive.

Standing up for your rights in the face of adversity is, of course, easier said than done. The best hope of modifying an intimidator is to adopt assertive behaviours and hang on to them come what may. Whenever, for example, your intimidator is unduly harsh and punitive you must draw yourself up to your full height, look them in the eye and say 'In my opinion you are being too harsh. My performance would improve if you were more supportive.' Whatever you say it must:

- be succinct (no longer than two sentences)
- point out what you think is wrong at present
- explain what you want to happen in future
- be capable of repetition (if need be you must repeat it over and over again and make no concessions).

If, after a number of repetitions, an assertive stance has no impact on your intimidator, you can at least learn from the experience by resolving never again to allow yourself to be intimidated by anyone. If you stand up to future attempts on a 'start as you mean to go on' basis, would-be intimidators will get the message and put you in their 'non-susceptible' category.

Judgemental

Judgemental people make a practice of being both judge and jury. They are prone to making unfavourable comparisons between people. Normally judgements go either way and are just as likely to be favourable as unfavourable, but judgemental people are quick to condemn. They have a set of values and beliefs that they apply to everyone. They moralise, criticise and disapprove.

If judgemental people kept their thoughts to themselves there would be less of a problem. Unfortunately they are only too keen to air their conclusions. They therefore deservedly gain a reputation for being opinionated and hard to please. The constant stream of critical judgements demotivates people who feel, with some justification, that they have been misunderstood.

THE OPTIONS

▶ Do nothing

You might feel daunted by the prospect of making any worthwhile impact on a dyed-in-the-wool judgemental person. But if you take no action, at least to correct judgements you know to be erroneous, miscarriages of justice are the inevitable consequence.

▶ Alter your perception of the problem

You could perceive judgemental people as self-imposed custodians of high moral standards. Without their constant critical surveillance, standards of behaviour would decline. Only judgemental people have the guts to speak out and prick people's consciences.

This idyllic perception is slightly marred by the tendency for judgemental people to wear their prejudices on their sleeves and jump too readily to biased conclusions. But perhaps that is a price worth paying to have honest people who aren't afraid to speak their minds even if it means upsetting people.

▶ Persuade the problem person to change

Judgemental people respond best to a direct approach. Calling a spade a spade is a way of life for them and they tend to despise innuendos, oblique approaches and anything 'diplomatic' (a derogatory term for them).

The challenge is to persuade judgemental people to do two things that they haven't yet mastered. First, to resist the temptation to jump to conclusions and secondly, to modify their outspokenness. The former is more difficult than the latter.

People who jump too quickly to conclusions do so because they suffer from a low tolerance for uncertainty and ambiguity. They feel uncomfortable without the security of an answer. Open-mindedness is anathema to them. The most feasible approach is to suggest that they work backwards from a conclusion they have reached to the evidence to validate it. This is somewhat topsy-turvy (it makes more sense to collect evidence and then use it to reach a conclusion), but at least it provides a practical starting point.

The gamble is that sometimes some of the evidence will contradict or challenge the conclusion already reached. The more this happens, the more it serves to demonstrate the tenuous nature of conclusions reached too hastily. Reassure the judgemental person that suspending judgement and retaining an open mind are but *temporary* stages *en route* to reaching a conclusion. There is nothing wrong with judgements, provided they can be held up to the light and substantiated.

Your second task is to convince the judgemental person that it is one thing to think a judgement and another to pronounce it. The crucial difference is that thoughts are unseen and can only be inferred from what is said and done, whereas pronouncements have a direct impact on people. Again, being practical, it might prove more feasible to persuade the person to bite their lip while they consider whether a pronouncement will help or hinder. They will protest that this smacks of censorship and dishonesty, but the acid test is whether a pronounced judgement will enhance someone's performance. If it has to be delayed for a palatability check so be it. Judgements that are rejected out of hand are of no use to anyone and erode the credibility of the judge.

▶ Modify the situation

Judgemental people must not be allowed to get away with it. There are at least two ways to change the situation so that they are compelled to be more helpful.

First, whenever they criticise resist the temptation to defend yourself and instead devote your energies to questioning them. Ask questions designed to understand the basis for the criticism and to extract positive ideas for improvement. The questions are not aimed at undermining or reversing the judgement, only clarifying it and forcing the judgemental person to go beyond it and produce helpful ideas. Having extracted their ideas, you are free to decide what to heed and what to discard. In the last analysis we are always our own arbiters.

Secondly, challenge the belief system and values behind the judgements. The idea is not to argue against the judgement, even is you disagree with it, but to bring to the surface the beliefs that give rise to it. This is tough because often beliefs, particularly long-held ones, are difficult to articulate and separate from gut feelings. But the beliefs are there somewhere and it is they that are doing the damage. Once beliefs have been expressed they become amenable to scrutiny and can be checked to see if they are still useful. All beliefs are, in a sense, conclusions that have been reached from experience and they tend too easily to become ossified. Fortunately they can be modified and updated and this is exactly what judgemental people are loath to do. There is nothing for it but to keep plugging away like water dripping on a stone.

Kowtower

Kowtowers behave in ingratiating ways – especially with anyone they regard as an authority figure. They tend to be deferential and to acquiesce rather than risk being disrespectful by saying what they really think or by disagreeing.

At first kowtowing may succeed in endearing the person to authority figures: they appear polite, compliant and co-operative. After a while, however, it tends to pall as the novelty of the fawning wears off and you start to wish that they would speak their mind and be more assertive.

Kowtowers are a problem because they are over-dependent on you to take the lead and make all the decisions. In slavishly following your lead, the kowtower fails to provide any added value; they are rarely forthcoming with ideas of their own and only ever agree with whatever ideas you have. Even an arrogant person begins to doubt that they can be right 100 per cent of the time! Deference is a serious problem in many hierarchical organisations because senior managers surrounded by yes-men lose touch with reality.

THE OPTIONS

▶ Do nothing

If you enjoy being surrounded by obedient lackeys, by all means do nothing. You will, however, be operating in a fool's paradise especially if you fall for the flattery and start to believe you are infallible. This is a recipe for complacency and sooner or later you are likely to get your come-uppance!

▶ Alter your perception of the problem

You could view your kowtower as being totally loyal; whatever you do and say, they will go along with you. After all, loyalty is generally regarded as a good thing and there isn't enough of it about nowadays! The problem is that kowtowers are unquestioning in their compliance and this should cause you to doubt the *quality* of their loyalty.

Alternatively you could perceive the kowtower as an ultra-polite person who leans over backwards not to cause offence. He or she has an opinion but would never dream of expressing it for fear of incurring the displeasure of someone more senior or more experienced. This perception would help you to understand that merely providing kowtowers with the opportunity to say what they really think is insufficient. Ways have to be found to make them speak their minds.

▶ Persuade the problem person to change

Assertiveness training could help kowtowers realise they have a right to express their opinions even, or perhaps especially, to authority figures. They need to discover that the ground will not open up and swallow them if they do something other than tug their forelocks and agree. But of course realising this and having the courage to do something about it are two different things. Initially the kowtower could be encouraged to practise being bolder in low risk situations. The discovery that their worst fears are not realised may encourage them to escalate their new-found boldness and try it on the people who really matter. They are likely to regress, however, if speaking their mind gets them into trouble at too early a stage in their struggle to be their own person. This is precisely why trying to modify the person without complementary modifications to the situation is expecting too much.

▶ Modify the situation

Kowtowers have learned to be deferential, probably over a long period, as they discovered that they had an easier time if they complied with the wishes of parents, teachers, policemen, bullies and other authority figures in their lives. However, what matters now is not past history but the current situation and how it continues, albeit unintentionally, to encourage kowtowing. Possible triggers for kowtowing are when:

- they are being instructed to do something by someone in authority
- everyone else appears to be in agreement
- it is possible to 'hide' in a large group or as a member of a committee.

Payoffs for kowtowing are:

- avoiding conflict, hassle, aggravation
- winning the approval of authority figures
- avoiding responsibility.

Kowtowing is often most in evidence when authority figures are present; remove them and the kowtowing either disappears or lessens. The main problem, therefore, is how an authority figure can reduce kowtowing without disappearing! The best hope is to change the triggers by continually putting the kowtower 'on the spot'. An obvious way to do this is to hold back on issuing instructions or giving your own opinion, and to invite the kowtower to produce an idea or opinion first. While they may still do this deferentially, by making them go first you have deprived them of something to agree with. Each time this is done, it is important to reinforce the behaviour by showing your approval and minimising conflict. In this way you can gradually entice the kowtower off the fence and cause them to discover that sticking their neck out doesn't after all mean that their head will get chopped off.

Lazy

Lazy people lack energy, often move in a lethargic way and, left to their own devices, do as little work as possible.

It is important to distinguish between people who are lethargic because they are ill, and therefore not *able* to move faster or work harder, and the shirkers who are perfectly able but *unwilling*. Laziness tends to be patchy in people who are fit but unwilling. For example, someone may radiate enthusiasm and appear far from lazy at a disco (or even when *talking* about the disco they went to last night), and this may contrast sharply with their laggardly approach to work. If you notice that their laziness comes and goes depending on the circumstances, then it is a problem of motivation. If it extends to everything they do then it is more likely to be a symptom of an illness and you should suggest that they see their doctor.

Lazy people are a problem because they do not produce sufficient work in a given time. If they work in an open-plan office or are part of a team effort they will often cause resentment among colleagues who are being inconvenienced by the laziness and are often having to produce more work themselves to compensate.

THE OPTIONS

▶ Do nothing

Lazy people will certainly hope that you will do nothing and let them continue to get away with low productivity! However, if they are not producing a fair day's work for a fair day's pay then you have no option but to do something. What you do depends on whether you are their colleague or their boss. Either way, you are likely to be adversely affected by their laziness and to want to do something about it.

▶ Alter your perception of the problem

The trouble with labelling someone as lazy is that it seems to be an all pervading personality trait with no obvious cure. Much more hopeful is to view it as a way of behaving which, like any other, is variable and has been learned. You could perceive the lazy person as 'street-wise' in the sense that they have discovered that dragging their feet on tasks they don't want to do means that they have to do less of them. Viewed this way you could conclude that there is no such thing as a lazy person, only someone who doesn't want to work. Ultimately what people want and don't want to do has to be their choice, but that doesn't absolve us from doing our best to influence their behaviour.

▶ Persuade the problem person to change

It is hard to convince someone that it isn't in their best interests to be lazy because all their experience points to the contrary. They have adopted laziness as a way of ensuring that they do less of what they don't want to do and, on countless previous occasions, they have got away with it. The acid test is to give them something they do want to do and see if the lazy behaviour continues. If their behaviour changes, it shows that the key lies in the tasks they are given, and that the person is not immovably lazy come what may.

The best course of action is therefore to change the situation and not to waste time counselling a lazy person. The only advantage in counselling someone is that it might provide useful pointers about how best to modify the situation to get them to be more productive.

▶ Modify the situation

No one, I have suggested, is lazy all the time – unless they are ill. They may be lazy at work but keen and enthusiastic when pursuing their hobby or some outside interest. Even while at work, it is likely that the laziness fluctuates to some extent between one activity or task and another. Triggers for lazy behaviour are usually found in the work itself. When tasks are uninteresting, repetitive or specialised to the point of being meaningless, people not surprisingly find it hard to maintain their enthusiasm and start to drag their feet. They can quickly get into the habit of moving slowly, procrastinating (see **Procrastinator**), chattering instead of working, and all the other behaviour patterns through which laziness manifests itself.

Payoffs for laziness are that people get away with doing less. In many jobs there are insufficient adverse consequences for low productivity. Unless they are paid on a piece-rate system, or their salary is performance-related, they still get the same pay. Tellings off fall on deaf ears (they may even be a welcome relief to the monotony) because the payoff for doing less work is stronger than the 'punishment' of being rebuked.

There are four strategies you can adopt to solve the problem. First you could examine the nature of the work itself to see if it could be made inherently more interesting. Can the work be less specialised so that the end result is meaningful? Can the drudgery of the same routine be broken up and varied in some way? Secondly, you could examine ways to remove discretion from the work so that the lazy person is forced to perform at the required pace. An assembly-line system, where the pace is set and the worker is compelled to work at the required speed, is a classic example. Of course people aren't happy with being automated like this, but it does wonders in reducing laziness.

Thirdly, you could pay people for results and not for attendance. Some system of performance-related pay could succeed in enticing the lazy person to increase their productivity. Fourthly, you could supervise the person's work more closely and instigate a system whereby they get to do something they like doing providing they have completed something they don't like doing. A 'sandwich' system breaks up the drudgery and builds in conditional rewards.

If none of these strategies is entirely possible, you might be able to combine parts of some of them. A combination of closer supervision, less discretion and the interspersing of carrots and sticks, for example, may well alter the situation sufficiently to banish lazy behaviour.

Manipulator

Manipulators are dishonest in the sense that they manoeuvre people into doing something that suits the manipulator more than the manipulated. Instead of making straightforward requests, manipulators engineer situations so that they get their own way. At the time, manipulated people invariably fail to realise that they are being tricked; only afterwards does the truth slowly dawn and resentment set in. The most obvious examples that spring to mind are when people have been manipulated into buying something they didn't really want or need, be it insurance, double glazing or a timeshare.

More subtle attempts to manipulate are a daily occurrence at work. Bosses manipulate subordinates, subordinates manipulate bosses and colleagues manipulate colleagues. For example, a boss may have given considerable thought to a particular problem and decided on the best course of action. Instead of coming clean he or she may choose to go through the charade of consulting the group, pretending that they are open minded and have no solution. The boss manipulates the conversation in such a way that the participants reach the same answer and are convinced that it is theirs.

Another example would be a subordinate manoeuvring their boss into agreeing to a course of action – perhaps to buy a certain type of equipment or to relocate the office or to bring in a particular firm of outside consultants – in such a way that the boss is convinced it was their own idea. Sometimes a manipulator can plot and scheme over a long period to bring about a particular outcome.

Manipulation is only a problem if people realise it has occurred and resent it. If manipulators are skilful enough to remain undetected then clearly it doesn't ever dawn on people that they have been tricked and there is no problem.

THE OPTIONS

▶ Do nothing

Manipulators manipulate because they find it an effective way to get what they want. If you do nothing it is inevitable that the manipulation will at least continue and probably increase. The more it succeeds, the more the tendency is reinforced. When you discover manipulative practices it is best to expose them for what they are, otherwise they can take hold and stifle authenticity.

▶ Alter your perception of the problem

You could see manipulators as skilled persuaders, with the patience of Job, who believe in winning people's commitment. This explains why they are keen to manoeuvre people into thinking that they, and not the manipulator, thought of an idea. You could even come to see it as altruistic on their part, or at least no worse than telling a white lie. Clearly this perception is not sustainable if the manipulation is transparent, either at the time or subsequently, and the victims become resentful.

▶ Persuade the problem person to change

The best way to change a manipulator is to call their bluff and confront them with their deviousness. Exposure is a shock to a manipulator who is unused to such straightforwardness. The chances are that without your help the manipulator isn't aware of their behaviour and its consequences. Manipulation will have become a way of life for them, an approach they slip into without considering any alternatives.

Use a recent example where you were manipulated or where you watched someone else being manoeuvred by the manipulator. Don't dwell on the subsequent feelings of resentment because the manipulator will probably dismiss those as a small and inevitable price to pay from time to time. A much more fruitful line is to establish what the manipulator's objective was and, in the light of that, identify a range of alternative approaches with the advantages and disadvantages of each. An alternative that the manipulator is unlikely to have given adequate, if any, consideration to is being utterly straightforward, open and honest. If you can demonstrate that their objective could have been more easily achieved via a direct route, you might succeed in getting straightforwardness on to their agenda. Help them to see that whenever they want to influence someone they have choices and that there is a time and place for an authentic straightforward approach and a time and place for manoeuvring and manipulation.

▶ Modify the situation

Manipulators have learned to manipulate because, in their experience, doing so invariably gets them what they want. You need, therefore, to work out how to influence the situation so that they more easily get what they want when they are straightforward and are thwarted when they choose to be manipulative. In other words, you need to manipulate the situation so that manipulation no longer succeeds. In order, however, not to be accused of being a pot calling the kettle black, you should do this openly by consulting the manipulator. Agree with them some inconvenient sanctions if they are caught being manipulative and some rewards for authenticity and straightforwardness. An excellent sanction might be that the manipulator has to go and confess and apologise to those they've manipulated. Openness of this kind is the antithesis of manipulation and would prove a salutary experience for a habitual manipulator. By contrast, rewards for straightforwardness could be thanks, extra co-operation and less hassle.

Martyr

Martyrs seek attention by making it clear that they are doing good deeds at considerable personal inconvenience. The good deeds are often quite simple things like volunteering to answer someone's telephone during the lunch break, or helping someone by letting them jump the queue for the photocopier, or giving a colleague a lift when their car has broken down. Favours such as these are volunteered with apparent willingness and accepted at face value. The martyr then proceeds to sigh and pass comments designed to leave the recipient in no doubt about the considerable self-sacrifice involved. Examples might be, 'Your phone never stopped ringing. I didn't even have time to eat my sandwiches'; 'By the time I got to the copier it had run out of toner'; or 'Coming this way will make me late for my appointment'. 'Poor me' remarks like these are never directly accusing. They aim to get the recipient to feel guilty and as a consequence to be lavish in their apologies and expressions of gratitude.

Real martyrs are sacrificed at the hands of others for a cause or principle. People who play at martyrdom sacrifice themselves as a manoeuvre to get other people to feel guilty. It is a psychological game (see **Gamesman**) which, when successful, has people feeling needlessly indebted and gradually distorts authentic 'give and take' practices.

THE OPTIONS

▶ **Do nothing**

Ignoring martyrs deprives them of their attention-seeking payoff and therefore removes any advantage in continuing with the game. Martyrdom may, however, be such an ingrained habit pattern that it obstinately carries on of its own volition long after it has been rendered obsolete. Ignoring it can do no harm and is certainly recommended, but by itself may not be sufficient to crack the problem.

▶ **Alter your perception of the problem**

You could perceive martyrs as under-valued and exploited people who put themselves out and receive little or no thanks. The act is a cry for appreciation, for a bit of loving care. They are willing, altruistic people who are continually taken for granted and used by others. Quite understandably, therefore, they play the martyr in order to win the sympathy and appreciation which is due to them and, it seems, cannot be secured in any other way.

This perception might help you see martyrdom as a cry for help and to be more fastidious in providing plenty of unconditional positive reinforcement, not just when it is asked for. Martyrs have a high need for positive 'strokes'. Martyrdom is a sure sign that they are below their stroke quota.

▶ **Persuade the problem person to change**

Martyrs suffer from low self-esteem and this makes them over-reliant on recognition from other people. You are unlikely to make much impact on the way they tend to see themselves, but you could take a more pragmatic approach and concentrate on demonstrating that there are more effective ways to win people's approval. The martyr's act follows a two-stage pattern: first, volunteering to help and, secondly, a spate of 'poor me' remarks. It is the volunteering tendency that makes it so easy for the martyr to be taken for granted. If help had to be requested *before* it was forthcoming, it increases the likelihood of thanks and appreciation. The act of asking for help is an admission that there is a problem and that the martyr is being sought out as someone useful who can help to solve it. If profuse thanks were offered after the martyr had come to the rescue then 'poor me' remarks designed to engineer thanks would no longer be necessary.

The key, therefore is to persuade martyrs to take a calculated gamble by not volunteering and instead waiting to be asked. If they jump the gun by volunteering, counsel a little self-flagellation by encouraging them to resist the temptation to indulge in 'poor me' appeals for gratitude.

▶ **Modify the situation**

Martyrdom may well have been perfected over a long period. Breaking the habits of a lifetime by willpower alone requires a superhuman effort. Anything you can do to modify the situation so that martyrdom is made difficult or less successful will be helpful.

A preventative measure is to go out of your way to lavish praise, encouragement and anything else that conveys recognition and appreciation on the would-be martyr. This meets their 'stroke' quota without the need to play games. A remedial measure is to withhold these eminently desirable payoffs whenever 'poor me' invitations are extended. If the martyrdom has been openly discussed and exposed as a crooked way to get appreciation, you could make a point of reminding the martyr as and when they indulge. A simple 'there you go again' may be sufficient to raise their self-awareness and get them consciously to intervene.

Meddler

There are people who have 'itchy fingers' and suffer from a strong compulsion to meddle. They find it difficult to let go and delegate. This happens because they pride themselves on being able to do things rather better than anyone else.

Meddlers tend to excel when it is appropriate to produce results themselves but to become a menace when it is their job to get results through other people. They fail to make the transition from being a hands-on operator to being a manager. They tend, therefore, to rush around being dynamic, having a finger in every pie, interfering with the way people are doing things and generally keeping everyone on a short rein. The worry is that meddlers tend to get promoted partly because they once excelled as operators and partly because of their high visibility. Unfortunately they make poor managers unless they are in a dire situation that needs drastic action to turn it round. Interventionists make excellent trouble-shooters but poor consolidators.

If you work for a meddling boss it is a problem for you because you are never trusted to get on with something in your own way. Their interventions can take many forms, of course, and may be direct to you or may extend to your subordinates and other people. The interventions might take the form of checking progress, or be more substantial, where the goal posts are moved. Meddlers are often inconsistent and change their minds on a whim (see **Impulsive**).

Over time it is likely that you will gradually buckle under and become increasingly dependent on your interventionist boss. This is an entirely understandable reaction, since interventionists tend to make

121

life difficult for people who do not comply (usually by meddling more, not less!).

THE OPTIONS

▶ Do nothing

Taking no action is the equivalent of resigning yourself to continued interference. There is a slim chance that your meddling boss will learn to trust you and intervene less, or that someone else will become the primary focus of their unwanted attentions. It certainly helps to have a few less competent colleagues who keep the interventionist busy while you get on with things.

A more positive approach is to do something about some interventions and nothing about others. You could target the interventions that you find most irksome and learn to accept the others.

▶ Alter your perception of the problem

Instead of seeing your boss as an interfering busybody you could see them as someone who is genuinely interested in what you are doing. As far as they are concerned their interventions are designed to be helpful not irksome. Their heart is in the right place and they might be horrified to discover that you find their attentions a pain.

If you regard your interventionist boss as taking an interest in you you will be inclined to manage him or her better. For example, you could make it your business to invite their involvement before they imposed it upon you. In this way you could take the initiative and channel their interest in certain areas of your activities while keeping them clear of others.

▶ Persuade the problem person to change

Start by compiling a list of recent interventions, going back over the last month or so. It is important that they are all recent examples, rather than old ones, to avoid the impression that you are crying over spilt milk. Then for each intervention on your list work out the adverse consequences you experienced. Examples might be, 'I had to rewrite substantial parts of a report, and this resulted in its late delivery'; 'I was deprived of an opportunity to see the job through to completion'; 'I looked foolish and inept in front of the customer'; 'My subordinates gained the impression that my position was being usurped', and so on. The more evidence you have the better.

Now you are ready to confront your boss. Do this in an unemotional matter-of-fact way. The objective is to convince them that you would perform better if they meddled less or did it in a less public way, thus reducing the adverse consequences. Explain that you quite understand why, from their point of view, they like to keep their hand in by doing things you should be doing for them. Suggest that it would be a considerable help to you if, at the time you were given a task to accomplish, your degree of freedom was made explicit. You could, for example, suggest a simple way of indicating the extent to which something had been delegated to you by having a four-category system such as:

1 just do it
2 do it and tell me afterwards
3 plan it but check with me before you do it
4 consult me before you plan it.

If the level of delegation is made explicit at the time it is easier for you to challenge your boss if and when he or she subsequently meddles inappropriately. The long-term aim is to wean them off restricted delegation at levels 3 and 4 and move them increasingly to fully fledged delegation at levels 1 and 2.

▶ Modify the situation

Meddlers intervene because they have learned to do so in certain circumstances. You need to analyse the situation to understand why they meddle and to discover possible ways to change it so that they 'let go' more.

First answer the question, *when* do they meddle? Possible answers might be:

• when they are under pressure to deliver

- when the task is something that coincides with their own areas of expertise
- when complaints or signs of inadequacy are made known to them
- when you attempt to go it alone and leave them in the dark.

Secondly, answer the question, '*What do they gain* by meddling?' Possible answers might be that:

- they are in a better position to stave off pressure
- the job is done better (either in fact or in their perception)
- complaints and inadequacies are reduced
- they are able to give first-hand answers to awkward questions.

Once you have identified the triggers and payoffs surrounding their meddling you are in a position to examine the situation to see what you could modify. For example you could go it alone less and actively involve them more. They would then meddle on your terms rather than on theirs. If you know they have expertise, you could tap into it and thus channel the meddling so that it happens earlier in the process and is a useful contribution (eleventh-hour meddling is usually less helpful than timely interventions at an early stage).

Nagger

Naggers badger, cajole and pressurise people until they capitulate. Nagging is a behaviour that goes on relentlessly until it succeeds. In a rather perverse way it results in a win-win outcome: the naggers eventually get their way and the nagged are rewarded with a short respite before nagging recommences.

Nagging is a problem because it is a negative way to motivate people – it gets people to do things under duress rather than willingly. Henpecked people tend not to take the initiative and to become dependent on the nagging as a necessary spur to action. They may dislike it, and probably grumble about it, but nagging, once established, rapidly becomes institutionalised and prevents people from taking responsibility for their own actions. It is the equivalent of having quality-control inspectors who raise quality standards by what amounts to persistent nagging, as opposed to quality assurance that encourages everyone to be responsible for their own quality. Nagged people tend, therefore, to do the minimum to get the nagger off their backs, albeit temporarily.

THE OPTIONS

▶ Do nothing

This is a risky strategy, but if you are defiant and refuse to capitulate, nagging loses its potency and will gradually diminish. Clearly you would have to withstand the wrath and frustrations of the nagger and refuse to crack under the pressure that would no doubt be brought to bear. In reality, you might not be in a position to ignore the nagging and go your own sweet way, in which case read on to see if other options strike you as more feasible.

▶ Alter your perception of the problem

You could see nagging as a totally justifiable behaviour. If we define nagging as the repetition of the same request, it presumably only occurs when a request has not been met. If things were done after the first request, nagging would become redundant. This could help you to see that you get the nagging you deserve.

Naggers have other commendable attributes that you may not appreciate. For example, they are consistent, tending to have pet foibles that feature over and over again in their nagging. (Invariably these foibles are not shared by other people otherwise nagging to get them done wouldn't be necessary.) Naggers also have excellent memories and tend to recall precise details of when they asked who to do what.

▶ Persuade the problem person to change

You could always try nagging naggers not to nag! Unfortunately you will meet resistance because they are quite convinced that nagging works and is necessary. A more fruitful approach might be to avoid a full-blown attack and instead to concentrate on getting the nagger to reconsider priorities. Often nagging appears petty because it targets small things that are hardly cataclysmic if they aren't done. Things like turning lights out, keeping a door locked, making cheap-rate phone calls, using both sides of pieces of paper or recording the date and time on messages can escalate into matters of principle and assume an exaggerated importance. The nagger's motto might be 'It's the little things that count.' So try persuading them to reserve their nagging for the things that really count and to shrug off lesser issues or, better still, work out how to build them into the system so that they aren't reliant upon nagging. The idea is not to banish nagging but to make it rarer and therefore more likely to have impact. Things might get done on the second or third time of asking rather than the umpteenth.

▶ Modify the situation

If you are suffering at the hands of a nagger there are two ways open to you to prevent it (prevention being better than cure). First, list the things that the nagger nags you about. You should be only too well aware of them so it shouldn't be too much of a chore. Scan your list for recurring themes. Then work out how to do these *before* being nagged. This is the equivalent of preventative maintenance – you fix something before it needs fixing. Keeping one step ahead will certainly take the wind out of the naggers's sails.

Secondly, aim to do what the nagger asks *at the first time of asking.* This nips nagging in the bud by making it unnecessary for the nagger to repeat the request. If other commitments make it impossible for you to carry out the task straight away, tell the nagger when you will do it and then when you have done it.

You may well object that these two courses of action play right into the hands of the nagger. And you might be right. A more subtle plan is to commit yourself to doing what the nagger has asked, not immediately but a few days later. If during the waiting period, the request is repeated, then explain that you are postponing the action and put it back by a few more days. If, on the other hand, the request is not repeated during the waiting period, and the temptation to nag is resisted, then carry out the action as originally promised. This tactic punishes nagging, through postponement, while rewarding non-nagging. Obviously you can only employ this approach if your relationship with the nagger permits a combination of openness and downright cheek!

Overpowering

Overpowering people are energetic and bombastic. They are larger than life characters who enjoy being the centre of attention. Bombastic behaviours could include all or some of the following:

- talking or laughing loudly
- talking at length
- talking over the top of other people
- interrupting people
- always having the last word.

The problem with overpowering people is that, colossus-like, they dominate. The dominated become subservient and over-dependent lackeys; they become *over*powered rather than *em*powered. Bombastic, domineering people always justify the necessity of their style by pointing out that they are surrounded by wimps. The chicken and egg conundrum is conveniently lost on them: which came first, the wimps or the bombastic style?

THE OPTIONS

▶ Do nothing

This is undoubtedly the easiest option. If it doesn't happen too often, and if you are not being seriously inconvenienced, you could always admit defeat, give in gracefully and lie back and enjoy the experience of being overwhelmed. This, the easy way out, may suit you and will certainly suit the domineering person. In their eyes you join the wimps and require 'strong leadership' (a euphemism for dominating people).

▶ Alter your perception of the problem

You could see overpowering people as colourful, flamboyant characters brightening an otherwise drab world. Encounters with these larger than life characters are eventful and far from boring. They keep you on your toes and provide the raw material for countless amusing anecdotes. They may not be the easiest people to live with, but they certainly make life interesting.

▶ Persuade the problem person to change

Unless you are at least as powerful as the overpowering person, you haven't a hope of persuading them to mend their ways. You'd be better off working on the overpowered, helping *them* to find ways to cope with their feelings of awe or be more assertive (see **Kowtower** and **Reserved**). Bombastic, domineering people are convinced that they are right and all their experience tells them that the world is biased in their favour. They are more likely to be noticed and to get promoted than the meek and mild. Even if they attend a interpersonal skills course and discover collaborative behaviours such as listening to other people and reaching 'we' decisions, they continue to harbour considerable reservations about grey compromises, being reduced to the lowest common denominator and generally losing out to the wimps. Unconvinced, they soon return to their bombastic ways unless the 'wimps' have succeeded in rising to the occasion and impressing with their contribution. But that brings us to the next option.

129

▶ Modify the situation

Since bombastic people are invariably impervious to suggestions that they should quieten down and be less flamboyant, working out how to modify the situation is a more practical approach. As ever, it is important to be realistic and to decide precisely what aspect of their behaviour you most want to modify. Plan to tackle one aspect at a time. It could, for example, be hogging the conversation so that you can't get a word in edgeways. Now work out what you could do to create an opportunity to have your say. For example, you could:

- start speaking loudly when they pause for breath (even flamboyant people breathe)
- put up you hand and wave it vigorously
- gaze fixedly, preferably with a horrified expression, at a point somewhere behind the flamboyant person and start speaking as soon as they pause to see what is distracting your attention
- stand up suddenly and stay standing while you say your piece (standing while others sit is domineering)
- indulge in behaviours that show you are not listening – for example, look pointedly at your watch, stretch, yawn, look down and read your notes (this deprives the flamboyant person of an adoring audience and so they find it harder to keep going).

These ideas, and others like them, will create an opening. It is then vital that you say something worthwhile that will stand a chance of registering with the overpowering person. If you can't trust yourself to come up with something spontaneously then there is nothing for it but to have some pre-prepared offerings. At all times, your aim is to gain the respect of the bombastic person so that they value your contribution and listen to you more.

Another useful tactic is to resolve to push yourself forward early on in the encounter. If you wait and succumb to the flamboyance it becomes more and more difficult to stir yourself into action. Listening is a relatively passive activity and the longer you do it the more the energy level drops. So make it a rule to get cracking within, say, five minutes or so. Once you have got in and said something, it becomes progressively easier to maintain the momentum.

Perfectionist

Perfectionists fret about getting things right. In this imperfect world they tend to be in a permanent state of dissatisfaction – both with their own efforts and with those of other people. Rarely do achievements match their impossibly high standards. They often invest a disproportionate amount of energy in getting small details right. This tendency to be pedantic means that they rarely bother with the big scene or anything 'macro'.

Perfectionists are a problem because, in striving to get everything right, they often produce their own work late and fuss unduly over other people's work. If you write a report or a letter they will fiddle with it or send it back to you covered in pernickety corrections. If you give a presentation they will point out a spelling mistake in your visual aid or some other insignificant blemish. These things distract attention from the real issues and waste time getting things corrected. No doubt perfectionists have their own cross to bear, but they certainly have a knack of inconveniencing those around them.

THE OPTIONS

▶ Do nothing

Whether you opt to do nothing depends on the extent to which you are inconvenienced. You might be able to shrug off your perfectionist's fussiness as a minor irritation or you might be driven to distraction by the constant quest to have everything 'just so'. If it is at the level where you can grin and bear it that's fine, but if you are caught up in the vicious circle of trying to satisfy a demanding perfectionist you will need to do something to stay sane.

▶ Alter your perception of the problem

You could view perfectionists as the custodians of a zero-defects policy. This would help you to see them as admirable people with high standards that are worth striving for even if, as fallible human beings, we are sometimes found wanting. 'Aim high and you hit high' goes the old saying, and perfectionists are reminders of the need to raise our sights and refuse to settle for second best. Looked at this way we all stand to gain from our encounters with perfectionists. The fact that they are never likely to be satisfied with our efforts is something we must regard as an endearing characteristic spurring us on to greater heights.

▶ Persuade the problem person to change

Perfectionism is an obsession and it is unlikely that you will be able to talk someone out of it. Obsessions stem from deep seated and stubborn beliefs. Perfectionists believe it is right to strive for perfection and in a masochistic way, the more elusive it is, the more they feel compelled to double their efforts. Reassurances that something less than perfection will do fall on deaf ears. The only hope is if the perfectionist gets to the point where he or she wants to do something about it – because it is making *their* life intolerable! In this case you can help by getting them to overhaul the belief that things *must* be 100 per cent correct. Counsel them to banish the absolute 'must' and instead settle for a preference, even a strong preference, that things are error-free.

▶ Modify the situation

If we think of perfectionism not as a strong belief system but more as a pedantic way of behaving, it helps us to see the links between circumstances and the tendency. Fussy, pernickety behaviour is more in evidence on some occasions than on others. For example triggers for pedantic behaviour might be when:

- the person is an acknowledged expert and has a reputation to safeguard
- a written piece of work is destined for more senior people or will be read by customers
- the person spots certain spelling or grammatical mistakes
- someone over-confident needs to be brought down a peg or two.

Payoffs for pedantic behaviour might be that:

- the offending work gets corrected
- a stand is made on a matter of principle and the perfectionist 'cause' is advanced
- the perfectionist scores points
- people are put in their place or kept on their toes.

There is a straight and a crooked way to deal with perfectionists. You can either do the honest thing and redouble your efforts to produce error-free work, thus removing the triggers, or you can put in deliberate mistakes to give them something to find. The latter doesn't solve the problem, but at least it gives you some measure of control, leaves you less vulnerable and ensures that the perfectionist gets their payoffs while inconveniencing you less.

Pessimist

Pessimists fear the worst and have a gloomy outlook on life. Their philosophy is 'If something can go wrong, it will.' They are prophets of doom.

Pessimists can be a problem because they dampen other people's enthusiasm. Pessimists are 'can't do' people and they are therefore a drag in a 'can do' culture. They are difficult people to enthuse. While you explore the virtues of a given course of action they will react with warnings that it will never work. Their defeatist stance makes them difficult to motivate. Even when they are proved wrong, and events turn out well, their pessimistic outlook remains intact. Their reasoning is that you got away with it that time, but next time will be different.

Pessimists are also a problem because they find it extraordinarily difficult to trust others. Their pessimism leads them to expect the worst of people. This makes them extremely poor delegators; they can't bring themselves to believe that a delegated task will turn out well.

THE OPTIONS

▶ **Do nothing**

You may well be pessimistic about the prospects of doing anything to modify a staunch pessimist! If you can't beat them, join them! On the other hand, while you may not consider it practical to make significant inroads into their underlying *attitudes*, you might want to modify some of their manifestly pessimistic *behaviours*. You could settle for leaving them to *think* it can't be done, provided they don't actually *say* it.

▶ **Alter your perception of the problem**

You could see pessimists as a useful counterbalance to unfettered optimism. Pessimists make very good devil's advocates, and you could use them to test ideas to destruction. Somewhere between optimism and pessimism lie sensible courses of action. Without pessimists you might get carried away on a wave of optimism and live to regret it. This change in perception could help you to see that pessimists have a useful contribution to make. The secret is to have a mixture of optimists and pessimists, not one without the other.

If you tend to be an optimist (which is very likely if you regard pessimism as a problem), you could deliberately seek out a pessimist to be your mentor. The contrasting approaches could dovetail and prove that two heads really are better than one. The combination is a winner, even if the pessimist refuses to see it that way!

▶ **Persuade the problem person to change**

There is no point in trying to persuade someone to change their pessimistic outlook. It is unlikely that you will succeed, and in any case that's their business. It is more hopeful if you concentrate on modifying some of the behaviours that result from the basic attitudes.

Make a list of the pessimistic behaviours that are a problem for you. Examples might be:

- saying negative things such as 'It's bound to go wrong'; 'It won't work'; or 'It can't be done'
- resisting change
- saying 'I told you so' when things haven't worked out
- distrusting strangers and anyone who hasn't served a long apprenticeship and earned the right to be trusted.

Having got your thoughts straight about the behaviours that are a problem, find an opportunity to sit down with the problem person and show them the list. Reassure them that you quite understand that they have a right to maintain a pessimistic outlook on life and that this is their choice. But explain how the behaviours have an adverse affect on you or other people, preferably providing examples from recent experience. Invite them to put the behaviours in order from easiest to most difficult to change. Finally concentrate on helping them plan how they are going to reduce the occurrence of the behaviour they have selected as the easiest to change.

Starting with the easiest first is deliberate. It is likely to help pessimists become more optimistic about the chances of success as well as making success more likely. There may well be a 'domino effect', with other behaviours on the list also diminishing, or you may have to move down the list tackling each behaviour one by one over a period of time.

▶ Modify the situation

It requires considerable effort to modify an outward behaviour while an underlying attitude is pulling in the opposite direction. Adjusting the situation to make it more supportive to the change is an enormous help. Pessimists may have a permanent predisposition to pessimism but they only behave pessimistically on certain occasions. The key to changing the behaviour is to understand what circumstances bring on a pessimistic reaction.

Possible triggers for pessimistic behaviours are when:

- changes are proposed out of the blue with no prior consultation
- some risky future event is being discussed that could easily go wrong
- the pessimist is meeting people for the first time
- they are dealing with people who have not been trustworthy in the past.

Some of these triggers are presumably unavoidable; no one can go through life without encountering strangers or people who have let you down in the past. However, the triggers do offer a ray of hope. It could help to reduce pessimism if, before a change, there was gentle consultation. This would give the pessimist time to adjust and to identify the plus points. You could artificially reverse the roles and offer to play devil's advocate yourself and get them to accentuate the positive.

Possible payoffs for pessimistic behaviours are:

- playing safe and avoiding the risk of being wrong
- being able to say 'I told you so'
- avoiding disappointment.

The payoffs help us to appreciate that pessimism offers protection from the wicked world. It is a way of playing safe. It is therefore essential not to deprive the pessimist of their payoffs and expose them to undue risk. When they are more optimistic and when they are brave enough to nail their flag to the mast you must support them through thick and thin. Otherwise it is predictable that they will take the easy option and retreat into cosy pessimism.

Plagiarist

Plagiarists take other people's ideas, inventions and writings and pass them off as their own. Imitation may be the greatest form of flattery but it doesn't feel like it when you discover that your work has been copied with no acknowledgement. In practice it is often difficult to draw a line between learning from someone (a 'good' thing) and stealing from someone (a 'bad thing'). Learners tend to add something of their own to whatever they have taken and to be generous in their acknowledgements. Plagiarists on the other hand are copycats; they merely reproduce and reiterate without added value (they may change some words here and there to make it appear different, but this is purely cosmetic), and they neglect to mention any of their sources.

Plagiarism is a problem because it destroys trust and cooperation. People who are robbed of the recognition they deserve often have strong feelings of outrage and hostility. Plagiarism is a form of exploitation and victims can change from being open and willing (essential to aiding the learning process) to being secretive and suspicious (a serious inhibitor to the learning process). It is not unknown for the victims of plagiarism to become so paranoid that they stop producing original work and become preoccupied with the protection of what they have already produced.

THE OPTIONS

▶ **Do nothing**

This option plays right into the hands of plagiarists. They would love you to go on churning out work that they can pinch and pass off as their own. You cannot afford to be submissive.

▶ **Alter your perception of the problem**

You could see plagiarists as enthusiasts who are swept along and in their excitement forget the original source of their ideas. Plagiarists are like magpies constantly on the look-out for ideas to add to their collection. They often excel at packaging and presenting ideas more successfully than the originators.

If you view plagiarists as enthusiastic collectors it may help you to feel less bitter about their antics. You might even be charitable enough to believe that they would have given you credit if only they had remembered their sources. Seen in this light, plagiarism is careless rather than vindictive.

▶ **Persuade the problem person to change**

Plagiarists have to be confronted and left in no doubt that you take a dim view of their failure to give credit where it is due. Realistically you can probably only appeal to their sense of fair play and try to shame them into being more considerate. It helps if you can convince them that acknowledging indebtedness to other people takes none of the kudos away from them as the presenter of the ideas. In fact, being seen to be generous with credits is likely to *enhance* the plagiarist's reputation. Clearly a hardened plagiarist, anxious to find every opportunity to impress, will find this hard to accept. Persuade them to test this out next time they write a report or give a presentation by being punctilious in acknowledging the contributions of others. At worst it will make no difference to their credibility; at best it will greatly enhance it. They need a lot of help, however, if they are to make this discovery.

▶ Modify the situation

Plagiarists plagiarise for two reasons. First, it is far easier to pinch other people's ideas than to produce original work (plagiarists put a gloss on this by pointing out the absurdity of reinventing the wheel). Secondly, more often than not, they get away with it. If plagiarists were pilloried every time they failed to give due acknowledgement, you can be quite sure that they would never have become hardened plagiarists in the first place.

It probably isn't feasible to make plagiarism impossible, but you can at least work out how to make it more difficult. For example you could:

- put your ideas in writing instead of just saying them in conversation; it is easier to 'prove' plagiarism from the written than the spoken word
- make sure your name and the date are conspicuously displayed on everything you write; this doesn't prevent their deliberate removal but at least it guards against absent-minded plagiarism
- be careful to circulate your ideas to a number of people so that if they are plagiarised at least you will not be alone in knowing this has happened; someone else may blow the whistle on the plagiarist and save you the trouble.

After each incident of plagiarism it is essential that you register your disapproval with the plagiarist and never relax your assertive stand. You must also seek out opportunities to put the record straight with people who may have been hoodwinked into believing it was the plagiarist's own work. This must be done in a straightforward, matter of fact way lest it seems you protest too much or are overly sensitive. You may feel hard done by and indignant but it will not help to show this to anyone other than the plagiarist.

Prejudiced

Prejudiced people are unjustifiably and unreasonably biased. They are stuffed full of preconceived opinions which predetermine their reactions to people and events. Prejudices can roam uncontrolled over a wide spectrum from race and colour to creed and sex to age and apperance to behaviour and position.

Everyone is prey to preconceived opinions; they are handy in that they obviate the need to start from scratch each time a new set of circumstances is encountered. The problem with prejudiced people is that they fit the world to their opinions rather than the other way round and become the victims of their preconceptions without even realising it. If you know you are biased, you can take steps to counterbalance the bias. Prejudiced people don't do this. They are content to allow their unreasonable opinions automatically to influence their behaviour.

It is the equivalent of the tail wagging the dog. A sexist will therefore automatically discriminate against members of the opposite sex since in their opinion they are inferior. Likewise with a racist, an ageist and all other 'ists'. Quite understandably, unjustified discrimination causes resentment and accusations of unfairness and inequitable treatment. In the face of all this the prejudiced person remains relatively unperturbed, convinced that they are not prejudiced or that they are right and everyone else must be wrong.

THE OPTIONS

▶ **Do nothing**

If you are suffering at the hands of a prejudiced person, doing nothing is definitely not recommended. The lack of feedback will leave them serenely captivated by their prejudices and oblivious to any problems they may cause. Worse, unchallenged prejudices will become even more entrenched, while the prejudiced person gives credence to happenings that reinforce their correctness and conveniently discards data to the contrary.

▶ **Alter your perception of the problem**

Perhaps the only good thing that can be said about prejudiced people is that they are entirely consistent! While their prejudices dictate, their behaviour is predictable. Prejudiced people are not in the habit of moving the goal posts. This is useful because it means we are able to second-guess their reactions in advance. Forewarned is forearmed, and so we should never be surprised or caught on the hop.

▶ **Persuade the problem person to change**

There is nothing you can do or say that is guaranteed to have a lasting impact on the prejudiced person. People's prejudices are stubborn; they are part of a belief system that has successfully programmed the owner over many years and they are not going to be abandoned lightly.

Your best bet is to start with the outward behaviour that flows from an underlying prejudice and work backwards, checking the thought process that lies behind the behaviour. For example, suppose someone has rejected out of hand all male applicants for a secretarial position. You could gently probe the reasons for this piece of behaviour and discover that it stems from a belief that secretaries ought to be female. Once expressed, the 'ought' can be challenged to see if it is capable of justification. Even if it is shown to be unjustifiable, do not necessarily expect the prejudice to be dented. It is too easy for the prejudiced person to rationalise by saying 'OK, so *in this particular instance*, male applicants are as eligible as female applicants, but *generally speaking* females make better secretaries than males.'

The prejudiced person is always the final arbiter of whether or not to overhaul an internal bias or belief. From the outside you can only make it more likely that they will see the benefit of realigning a prejudice that gives rise to actions that are constantly queried.

▶ Modify the situation

Prejudices are beliefs which have been learned from experience and are sustained by experience. Change the experience and there is a real possibility that the belief will change. This happens by compelling a change in behaviour and hoping for the subsequent realignment of a belief which is no longer tenable. For example, if we made it mandatory that all secretaries from henceforth must be male, the prejudiced person would have no choice but to comply and in doing so may learn that male secretaries are every bit as competent as female ones. The belief that all secretaries ought to be female is now under severe strain and is probably not sustainable.

This is, of course, a version of positive discrimination where legislation forces people to do things they would not otherwise do as an educational process. This strategy is always something of a gamble, but entrenched prejudices ride roughshod over appeals to 'see reason'.

So examine the current situation to see if there is anything you can do to force the prejudiced person to behave in a way that contradicts their prejudice. If you decide you are powerless to alter the situation in this way, then you will have to fall back on persuasion. A combination of persuasion and situational pressure is more likely to have an impact.

143

Procrastinator

Procrastinators postpone until the eleventh hour, and often beyond it, something they know they have to do. It is not that they are necessarily lazy (see **Lazy**) because they will often busy themselves with other things during the period of postponement. These 'other things' are invariably smaller and easier to accomplish than the task which they must eventually tackle. For example, a major task like writing a report may be postponed by indulging in comparatively petty tasks like clearing the in-tray, or reading yet another book or journal on the off-chance that it might be relevant. Anything, it seems, to avoid making a start on the major task. Often people have rituals they must go through before they can get started. Creative people such as writers and artists will often compulsively go through fixed routines before facing the blank page or canvas and superstitiously maintain that these rituals bring them luck.

Procrastinators can be a problem because they often fail to produce work by an agreed deadline. An approaching deadline becomes the trigger to start rather than to finish producing the goods. Procrastinators will claim (but they would, wouldn't they?) that the quality of their work is enhanced by leaving it to the last moment. They operate on a 'necessity is the mother of invention' principle. The drama they create by postponing a major task gets the adrenalin going and as a consequence procrastinators convince themselves that this is the best way to produce good-quality work.

THE OPTIONS

▶ **Do nothing**

Sometimes someone will be procrastinating but you will hardly be aware of it. Often procrastinators will move heaven and earth to get the job done even if it means staying up all night. In such cases you are unaffected by the procrastination habit. If, on the other hand, someone repeatedly produces major pieces of work late, it is worth investigating whether procrastination is a contributory factor.

▶ **Alter your perception of the problem**

You could perceive procrastinators as thoroughly worthwhile people who produce their best work when under pressure. If the pressure isn't already there, they create it by leaving things to the last moment. Perhaps procrastinators have got it right; maybe the best way to produce excellent one-offs that require originality and creativity is to work in a self-induced hot-house environment. Clearly this wouldn't be a sensible approach for routine tasks, but creative tasks may well benefit from the extra adrenalin released under pressure. This change in perception may help you to console yourself that it is worth waiting for.

▶ **Persuade the problem person to change**

Procrastinators are the sort of people who will readily admit that logically their behaviour is indefensible, but carry on doing it. They know full well that it isn't a sensible way of working, but sense doesn't come into it. So extolling the virtues of time management techniques is unlikely to rescue the hardened procrastinator. They will hear what you say, agree it makes sense and carry on with the procrastination habits. This is a classic example of where the intellect says one thing, only to have it over-ridden and cancelled out by the emotions. So counselling or training procrastinators is unlikely to make an impact in most cases. Their right brains will continue to dictate their working practices.

▶ Modify the situation

From a purely practical point of view, whether someone is a procrastinator or not is their business; what matters to you is that you receive good-quality work on time and are not inconvenienced by procrastination.

Triggers for procrastination are:

- a creative task to be tackled
- a negotiable, movable deadline
- a deadline that seems far off and apparently allows ample time to complete the job.

Payoffs that reinforce the tendency to procrastinate are:

- the excitement of the drama or crisis involved in getting the work done against hopeless odds
- better-quality work (real or imagined).

The way to change the situation so that procrastination does not result in late delivery is to tinker with the deadline. If, for example, the deadline is set earlier than the work is really required, it allows for some slippage. It is essential, however, that the procrastinator believes that the early deadline is the real one. If they get an inkling that it isn't, then the real deadline will continue to dictate their behaviour.

Another obvious technique to reduce the perils of procrastination is not to put all your eggs in one basket by having one final deadline, but to break the job up and have a series of deadlines. Each mini-deadline triggers an interim review of progress thus forcing the procrastinator to fragment their procrastination rather than saving it all up for a mega-procrastination.

If all else fails you could spring jobs on them, with a ready-made 'impossible' deadline, so that they have to buckle down and do it immediately. If procrastinators operate on the assumption that necessity is the mother of invention, at least you get to control the 'necessity' rather than leaving it to the whims of the procrastinator!

Quarrelsome

Quarrelsome people are quick to pick an argument. At the least provocation, or on occasions with apparently no provocation, they say something critical that sparks an adverse reaction. It is as though they have antennae scanning their surroundings actually looking for an argument. If one doesn't come to them in the natural course of events, they make one out of nothing. Quarrelsome people seem to be incapable of letting sleeping dogs lie. They challenge what they see as injustices, inadequacies and inaccuracies. For them everything rapidly becomes a matter of principle or a point of honour, and they find themselves unable to back down. In the eighteenth century they would have come to grief in a duel.

Quarrelsome people can be a problem because they have everyone on tenterhooks waiting for the next altercation. People aren't at their most productive if they are constantly looking over their shoulders preparing to defend themselves against the next peevish attack.

THE OPTIONS

▶ **Do nothing**

They say it takes two to argue so if you refuse to rise to the bait the
quarrelsome person is deprived of a sparring partner and there is no
contest. At a stroke you have solved the problem of having them pick
arguments with you. Unfortunately in their frustration at being
deprived, they are more likely to pick fights with other people. So,
unless you can persuade everyone to do nothing in the face of provocation, quarrelling will continue; albeit not with you.

▶ **Alter your perception of the problem**

You could see the quarrelsome person as someone who is in a permanent state of dissatisfaction and is therefore given to speaking up and
challenging what people say and do in a bid to bring about improvements. So their hearts are in the right place, it is just that they go about
things in an abrasive way.

Challengers are valuable people to have around, so long as you don't
take it personally and can handle their tetchiness. They are the sort of
people who have high standards which they are not prepared to compromise (for people like this 'compromise' is a dirty word).

This perception may help you see how you could use a quarrelsome
person as an agitator for change; they do the agitating, leaving you to
pick up the pieces and do the rest.

▶ **Persuade the problem person to change**

Let us be charitable and assume that the quarrelsome person speaks up
honestly and says what they really think without intending to pick an
argument. The situation degenerates into an angry exchange because
they challenge in a way that provokes a hostile reaction. They clearly
need to be counselled so that they understand how behaviour breeds
behaviour and that there are more effective ways to challenge than to
pick an argument. The chances are that, from their perspective, they
are blaming everyone else for not being able to 'take it'. Challenge
them to take responsibility for the way people react. Get them to keep a

score card where they give themselves a minus score for arguments and a plus score whenever their challenges are accepted or actively considered without rancour. Suggest that you meet after a month or so to analyse the results of this self-monitoring and to review their conclusions on the approaches that have worked best.

▶ **Modify the situation**

You need to appreciate *when* your quarrelsome person quarrels before you can see what aspects of the situation you could alter to reduce the disputes. Is it just a matter of them getting out of bed on the wrong side and feeling argumentative, or are there circumstances that crop up to stimulate their tetchiness? You could explore a number of possible triggers such as:

- the topic; have they got axes they regularly grind?
- the person; are there certain people they quarrel with and, if so, what is it about their behaviour that irritates the problem person?
- the time and place; is there a pattern or any discernible common denominators about the physical circumstances?

Each trigger you identify may produce ideas on how the situation could be changed to prevent quarrelsome behaviour. It is also worth considering the 'buzz' that arguing may give the problem person. Perhaps they enjoy the cut and thrust of a good argument. Perhaps they have a compulsion to win. Perhaps they like being the centre of attention and revel in the fact that they have got people on tenterhooks. Be wary of depriving the quarrelsome person of all their payoffs. You could have occasional sparring matches where you argue amicably. You could go for win-win outcomes rather than win-lose ones. Argue on your terms, not always on theirs; you choose the time, the place and the topic.

Reserved

Reserved people leave you to take all the initiatives in a conversation and hide their own light under a bushel. If you are an extrovert it is likely that you avoid introverts, preferring to mix with kindred spirits who are more gregarious and with whom you feel more at ease and have more fun.

Reserved people are a problem for you because they often have good ideas but hesitate to volunteer them. Shy people censor their own ideas before they say them, fearing that they are flawed and will not be received well. Unfortunately more ebullient, noisy people tend to assume that reserved people are not coming up with ideas because they don't have any. They therefore fill all the silences, produce ideas themselves, talk nineteen to the dozen and fail to encourage reserved people to join in.

The irony is that reserved people make extroverts more extroverted, and extroverts make reserved people even more reserved! The gap between them therefore widens, making it difficult for them to meet halfway. The reverse happens if you separate the reserved from the ebullient; the reserved come out of their shells and talk more and the extroverts find it impossible to get a word in edgeways and are forced to introduce some disciplines as an antidote to the chaos. This helps us to see that reserved people are capable of being more forthcoming when conditions are favourable.

THE OPTIONS

▶ **Do nothing**

If you do nothing it is predictable that reserved people will stay reserved. This is a relatively risk-free behaviour for them to retain and they are therefore unlikely to do anything to alter it themselves. Just occasionally you may get a glimpse of what you are missing when they unexpectedly produce a gem of an idea or say something really insightful. But apart from this, you are unlikely to have much of an incentive to put yourself out. The world is biased in favour of extroverts and if you are one of those you will tend to under-value the introverts and leave them to their own devices.

▶ **Alter your perception of the problem**

You could see reserved people as deep thinkers who have an essential contribution to make. Your mission would be to bring out their thoughts and use them to supplement your own less adequate ones.

This change in perception would make you more likely to lean over backwards to extract value from reticent people. You would do this by slowing down, asking open-ended questions, tolerating silences and, despite disappointments, maintaining an expectation that it's all there and it's up to you to tap into it.

▶ **Persuade the problem person to change**

Counselling reserved people is a delicate business because there is a risk that it will increase their self-consciousness and thereby exacerbate the problem (see **Self-conscious**). A gentle, non-directive approach is therefore essential. One of the most fruitful lines to take is to get the person to acknowledge that they often have an idea but hesitate to offer it, only to find that the moment has passed as someone else's inferior idea gains acceptance. This experience helps them to see that their idea was fine but that their hesitation deprived other people. Shy, reticent people rarely see their behaviour in this way and the realisation that they are selfishly depriving others can be quite a shock.

The counselling session can then concentrate on a plan of action that the reserved person can cling to on selected occasions. One idea is to encourage them to suspend self-judgement of their ideas by playing the blurting game. This has parallels with brainstorming where any idea, however half-formed or wild, is welcome. The idea is to get the reserved person to blurt out their idea *as soon as they have it.* You then positively discriminate in favour of blurted ideas by developing them. The blurting game can be used in the counselling session itself as a means of developing ideas about how to be more forthcoming!

▶ Modify the situation

No one is reserved and reticent every single waking moment. It might seem like it to you, but perhaps that's because of you! Reserved people are reserved in certain situations and much more forthcoming in others. So you need to discover what it is about the situation that is encouraging their reticence. Triggers for reserved behaviour might be when:

- there has been no time to marshall thoughts or do any preparation
- everyone is talking nineteen to the dozen
- strangers are present
- senior people are present.

Payoffs for reticence might be:

- avoiding ridicule or rejection
- maintaining the illusion of wisdom
- other people taking risks and making fools of themselves
- less to do (on the basis that the most vociferous are more likely to get 'volunteered' to carry out subsequent actions).

These triggers and payoffs help us to see how we could change the situation. For example, reserved people are likely to be less reserved if they are given time in advance to ponder the topic and gather their thoughts, and are not pressurised to come up with spontaneous ideas. They are also likely to be more forthcoming in situations where no senior people or strangers are present. So far as payoffs are concerned, it is vital to support ideas from reticent people and to avoid anything resembling criticism. They have to be helped to discover that their worst fears are not confirmed when they take risks. Gradually, as they become more ebullient, even the presence of seniors and strangers will not cramp their style. The payoffs also help us to see that it is important to give *more* jobs to reserved people if they have been reticent, *fewer* if they have joined in and met you halfway.

Sarcastic

Sarcastic people make humorous remarks at the expense of others. Sarcastic statements draw attention to people's weaknesses and are said with heavy irony. Examples are 'Thank you for that contribution, John, just what we needed', when the reverse is the case, or 'Oh brilliant, simply brilliant' when someone has just made a mistake, or 'Early again I see' when someone has arrived late.

Remarks like these are made deliberately with the intention of hurting someone and undermining their self-respect. Sarcasm is reputed to be the lowest form of wit, but that doesn't prevent it being prevalent in many work places. It can be a problem when it succeeds in getting to people and, even when it is passed off as friendly banter, it is a sign of competitive rather than cooperative relationships.

THE OPTIONS

▶ Do nothing

Ignoring sarcastic remarks deprives the person of the pleasure of any reaction. Over time the lack of any worthwhile reaction may get them to give up on you and reserve their teasing for worthier causes. There is a danger, however, that sarcasm has become so habitual that ignoring it will have no discernible effect. It is worth trying not reacting for a period, but it is likely to be a difficult tactic to sustain and may not do the trick. It may help to remind yourself of the old saying, 'Sticks and stones may break my bones but words can never hurt me.' Not, that is, unless you choose to let them.

▶ Alter your perception of the problem

You could perceive sarcasm as a sign of acceptance. Sarcastic people tend to indulge when they are feeling relaxed and comfortable in someone's presence so, far from getting upset, you could regard the remarks at your expense as an enormous compliment! The sarcastic person is pulling your leg because you are 'one of them', a friend not a foe and judged to be someone balanced enough to take it and give as good as you get.

This perception may help you to shrug off sarcasm as harmless and not be hurt by it or find it vindictive.

▶ Persuade the problem person to change

Sarcastic people will feign surprise that anyone could be affected by such innocent fun as the occasional sarcastic remark. They will be adamant that no offence is intended and that you are making a fuss about nothing. It is important, therefore, to be quietly assertive about the issue and not to be seen to over-react or dramatise. Simply tell them in a straightforward non-negotiable way that you would prefer it if they did not make sarcastic remarks and that you want it to stop. Back this up by resolving never again to allow a sarcastic quip within your hearing, whether directed at you or someone else, to pass without comment. Have a form of words worked out in advance so that you can swing into it effortlessly as the occasion demands. It might be 'Sarcasm is the lowest form of wit'; or 'Don't be sarcastic'; or 'Sarcasm isn't funny'; or 'Wit and sarcasm don't mix.' Anything short, punchy and to the point will do. Make sure it isn't sarcastic however, lest you be accused of the pot calling the kettle black!

▶ Modify the situation

Sarcastic people dish out cruel remarks for effect but they are usually selective in the sense that they direct them at certain people and not others. It is worth checking to see who the sarcastic person's victims tend to be. Are they junior? Do they react by showing that they are upset or by taking umbrage? If you are a victim, what is your relationship with the sarcastic person and how do you tend to react? It is also worth checking out the circumstances that trigger sarcasm. Does it occur when the victim has done something 'silly' and has laid themselves open to ridicule? In public to amuse an audience? Answers to these questions will help throw light on the circumstances that spark sarcastic remarks. You are then in a better position to explore the possibility of altering some aspect to make sarcasm less likely.

If you decide you are powerless to prevent sarcasm, then at least you can concentrate on ensuring that when it occurs it is not reinforced. The options we have already explored could all be useful: steadfastly ignoring it, or remarking on it every time it happens. Another splendid antidote to sarcasm is to take it literally and ignore the obvious irony. So when the sarcastic person says, 'Well done', assume they really mean it and react to it as if it were an authentic compliment. This is particularly irksome for the sarcastic person because it is the reverse of what they intended. Kept up over time, innocently blocking each sarcastic comment with a straight bat may exasperate them to the extent that they give up in despair!

Scatterbrained

Scatterbrained people are disorganised and forgetful. They tend to flit from one activity to another without following a consistent scheme or plan. They misplace things, often have untidy desks, and confuse details. A general lack of organisation pervades everything they do.

Scatterbrained people are a problem because they are unreliable. They cannot be depended upon to turn up at the right place, at the right time or with the right materials. Their hit-and-miss inconsistency is not only unnerving but often has a detrimental effect on the efficiency of other people. A scatterbrained boss, for example, involves people in a last-minute scramble to assemble essential details he or she requires for a meeting which has been in the diary for weeks. A scatterbrained colleague forgets to pass on vital messages or borrows your things because they have misplaced theirs (and then forgets to return them).

THE OPTIONS

▶ **Do nothing**

If you are not too seriously affected by the antics of the scatterbrained person, you could bide your time hoping that sooner or later they will no longer be able to tolerate the consequences of their own disorganisation and mend their ways. Unfortunately this could prove a forlorn hope. Scatterbrained people develop a high tolerance for chaos and disorder. If you tend to be a pernickety person who likes everything to be 'just so', you will find it impossible to appreciate the attractions of disorganisation. You are also likely to become exasperated by scatterbrained behaviour and to want to intervene in a bid to counteract the disorder.

▶ **Alter your perception of the problem**

You could see scatterbrained people as 'absent-minded professors' who have their minds on higher things. Scatterbrained people often make bright and entertaining companions, the source of many amusing anecdotes about the scrapes they get into as a result of their shambolic existence. If they live up to the stereotype they will come to work in odd socks, lock themselves out of their cars, carry off the wrong suitcase at airports, walk under ladders and disappear down open manholes. The world would be a duller place without its fair share of scatterbrained people.

It is also quite common for absent-mindedness to become something of an affectation, a whimsical attention-seeking display that over time has become habitual. This perception may help you develop more tolerance for scatterbrained people and be less inclined to write them off as just stupid or beyond rescue.

▶ **Persuade the problem person to change**

Scatterbrained people usually know that they are not as organised as other people but decline to make the effort to do anything about it. Organising themselves seems such a daunting uphill struggle that it is much easier not to bother. This inertia is compounded by the fact that they are unconvinced that there will be sufficient benefits once they have dragged themselves to the top of the hill.

The answer is to focus on aspects of their disorganisation that inconvenience *them*, rather than those that inconvenience *you*. This makes it more probable that they will be attracted to the advantages of making changes to their *modus operandi*. Also, concentrate on one or two aspects rather than everything all at once. This makes it seem less daunting and altogether more possible.

Once you have agreed what they would like to focus on, tease out their ideas on how to become more organised. If, for example, the problem concerns misplaced paperwork, the solution is likely to involve a simplified storage and retrieval system. If the problem is forgetting people's names, the solution is likely to involve an association technique to jog the memory. If the problem is forgetting commitments, then some sort of diary system or personal notice board is likely to prove helpful. The details of the plan will clearly differ depending on which aspect of disorganisation it seeks to tackle. Whatever the details, the plan must be tailor-made, specific rather than all-embracing and easy to implement.

Once the scatterbrained person has mastered some specifics and felt some benefits, they may be ready to progress to a course on self-management techniques where the merits of using a systematic personal organiser will no doubt be extolled.

▶ Modify the situation

You cannot force a scatterbrained person to become a paragon of organisation against their will. But you can examine the situation to see if existing systems could be tightened up or new ones put in place. Assume that the scatterbrained person is disorganised because the system allows them to be. The idea is to let the system take the strain. It may sound tedious, but you will have to enter the world of laid-down procedures, routines, checklists, places for everything, and so on. Bureaucracy should have been invented for scatterbrained people. If you haven't the authority to systematise their work, then at least you can dream up systems to minimise the inconvenience at the points where they impinge on you.

Alternatively you could aim for damage limitation by examining ways to reduce your dependence on the scatterbrained person. If, for example, you have to attend meetings together, conduct all the preparations as if you were going alone. This includes travelling arrangements as well as all the paperwork and other bits and pieces you require. Do not permit yourself to rely on them for *anything*. This helps to keep your blood pressure down and ensures that you emerge unscathed.

Secretive

Secretive people withhold information and keep other people in the dark. Sometimes this is justified. For example a delicate agreement might be placed in jeopardy if details were leaked before negotiations were completed, or unhelpful uncertainties might be provoked if sensitive information about a possible rationalisation, merger or acquisition were released before the way ahead was more certain. Or, more simply, perhaps the secretive person is honouring a request to respect confidentiality. At other times secretive behaviour is without justification and may deprive someone of the information necessary to carry out their function properly, to make the right decisions and so on.

Secretive people are a problem because, whether innocently or deliberately, depriving others of information seriously handicaps people's ability to contribute as effectively as they otherwise would. Uninformed people have no alternative but to depend on them as the fount of all wisdom (or to rely on the grapevine, which may be far from accurate). This has the effect of empowering the secretive person while ensuring that other people remain unempowered. Paradoxically the act of withholding information sends out a very clear message: you aren't trusted. Even where people obtain information from elsewhere, they often resent the endless games of cat and mouse.

THE OPTIONS

▶ **Do nothing**

If you believe that other people are responsible for keeping you informed, then you are more likely to be inclined to sit back and wait for it to happen. If, on the other hand, you believe that you are responsible for keeping abreast of events you are more likely to do something to ensure that you extract your money's worth from the secretive person. The latter is more constructive than the former.

▶ **Alter your perception of the problem**

It is possible that secretiveness stems, not from some sinister plot to marginalise you, but simply from absent-mindedness or carelessness. Perhaps your secretive person is busy but disorganised. They may forget that you need to know something or that you haven't been informed. If you turn it round the other way, you will appreciate how easy it is to imagine that when you know something everyone else does too and to be genuinely surprised to discover that this isn't so.

Of course, forgetfulness and carelessness are not adequate excuses, but at least this perception may help you feel less paranoid about the problem and more inclined to do something constructive to improve the channels of communication.

▶ **Persuade the problem person to change**

A nightmare scenario for secretive people is that they will have to spend all their time communicating to the detriment of other more interesting activities. Communicating is seen as a time-consuming and, worse, never-ending chore.

Secretive people often make the mistake of lumping all information together and failing to discriminate between that which it would be *nice* for people to know and that which people need to know. Nice to know is optional; *need* to know is essential. This discovery can be quite a relief to a secretive person for it helps to delineate what had previously been seen as an amorphous mass of information.

Persuade your secretive person to concentrate on communicating information in the 'need to know' category. Help them to define 'need to knows' as information people must have in order to make timely and informed decisions. Use your job as an illustration by drawing up a list of key decisions that are an integral part of your responsibilities and the information required to make those decisions. Don't make the list dauntingly long. Focus on, say, six key decisions rather than trying to cover everything. The shorter the list the more manageable it will seem to the secretive person. Make it a reciprocal process and compile a list of information it is essential you communicate to them to feed into their decision making. The lists can always be expanded when the flow of communication has been freed up.

▶ **Modify the situation**

Secretiveness stems from the fact that communicating information is a largely discretionary activity. Open people choose to communicate far more than secretive people, and it is the freedom to choose that is the root of the problem. The answer is to find ways to reduce the discretion so that communication is no longer a matter of choice. A formal system of briefing groups is a good example of this approach, where designated briefers are given information to pass on to their group as part of a cascading system throughout the organisation. Once you see the problem as one of too much discretion you might think of other ways to build communication into the system. Structured forms, E-mail, daily bulletins, bright yellow stickers, disseminating information during a coffee break or other occasion where people congregate are all possible methods. Don't reject them because they tend to be bureaucratic; if you suffer from secretive people, you need more bureaucracy not less.

Another way to change the situation is for you to work out the initiatives you need to take, perhaps on a daily basis, to keep yourself informed. It may seem obvious, but phoning the secretive person or calling in to see them and grilling them may do the trick. If you keep this up regularly you might even succeed in training them to inform you *before* you have to ask!

Self-conscious

Self-consciousness is more an internal feeling of inadequacy than a specific behaviour. People who are prone to the feeling tend to have low self-esteem and to be in a state of high anxiety about what other people think of their appearance or actions. This is because, in the absence of self-esteem, their esteem is totally dependent upon signals of approval from other people. No approval means they are robbed of any esteem.

Self-consciousness shows itself in a variety of submissive behaviours, such as being over-apologetic, self-deprecating, modest and embarrassed. Submissive people constantly underestimate their skills and abilities and need a disproportionate amount of tender loving care and encouragement. This saps your energy, takes time and can be exasperating if you have a low tolerance for over-dependent wimps. They are also a problem because there are certain tasks that cover them in embarrassed confusion. Any job they have to perform in public, such as giving a presentation of making a speech, is likely to be carried out in a self-conscious way.

THE OPTIONS

▶ **Do nothing**

If you steadfastly ignore self-conscious behaviours you deprive the person of the reassurance they are hoping for. Gradually therefore, their embarrassment in their dealings with you will be less evident but self-consciousness will undoubtedly remain in their dealings with other people. So doing nothing puts the behaviour 'on extinction', as behaviourists call it, but the internal feelings of low self-esteem will probably remain intact. Ignoring self-consciousness is certainly kinder than drawing attention to it.

▶ **Alter your perception of the problem**

Since self-conscious people are in a constant state of anxiety about what other people think of them, you could regard them as trustworthy souls who can always be relied upon to do their best to please. You could come to see their self-consciousness as a small price to pay for their conscientiousness.

▶ **Persuade the problem person to change**

Persuading someone that they needn't feel self-conscious is likely to exacerbate the problem rather than ease it. Self-conscious people already *know* they shouldn't feel self-conscious but in itself this does nothing to solve the problem. It's the equivalent of telling a worrier that there's no point in worrying!

The answer is to concentrate on one or two of the more troublesome behaviours rather than the internal feeling. People's feelings are their business; their behaviour is your business. Choose a behaviour that is detrimental to the person's job performance rather than one which might be irritating but is a peripheral issue. An example might be a display of undue modesty in a situation where utter conviction and confidence are called for. Provide examples of what you considered to be inappropriate modesty and see if they square with the perceptions of the self-conscious person you are trying to help. Fully acknowledge any feelings of inadequacy they express but don't get side-tracked, it's

165

the behaviour you are focusing on, not the associated underlying feelings.

Work out carefully what behaviours are needed to replace the modesty. This might mean rewording something that was said. For example, if a compliment had been paid to which the modest response was 'It was nothing really, if I'd had longer I could have done a better job', you could counsel the person to say 'Thank you' and leave it at that. (Reducing embarrassment and modesty usually means saying less not saying more.) Non-verbal behaviours may also be an important part of the recipe, for example increasing eye-contact (embarrassed people tend to look away while in the grip of the feeling).

The rationale for this focus on outward behaviours is 'If at first you can't make it, fake it.' If the wanted behaviours can be artificially induced there is a reasonable chance that, with practice, they will become more natural and the feelings of self-consciousness will gradually abate.

▶ **Modify the situation**

The difficulty with urging self-conscious people to over-ride their feelings and fake confident behaviours is that it puts all the onus on them to make the adjustments, even though they don't feel like it and nothing in the outward situation has changed. This is possible but it requires something of a super-human effort – especially for someone with low self-esteem. Much more helpful, therefore, is a combination of counselling together with supportive modifications of the situation.

The situational argument is that while self-conscious people are vulnerable to bouts of self-conscious behaviour, different situations trigger and reinforce them. Examples of triggers for self-consciousness might be when:

- the person is making a presentation or speaking
- they are doing something new or unfamiliar in front of an audience
- they realise they have just made a *faux pas*
- someone has violated their rights and assertiveness is called for.

Payoffs reinforcing self-conscious behaviour might be that:

- people back off and give the embarrassed person an easier time
- people counteract modest or self-deprecating comments by talking the person up and being more complimentary than they otherwise would have been.

If it were possible to keep self-conscious people away from other people the problem would be solved at a stroke! Short of banishing them to a desert island, some helpful modifications to the situation are possible. The aim should be to reduce unexpected events to a minimum and this can only be done by getting self-conscious people to prepare thoroughly and carefully rehearse what they are going to say. They are perfectly capable of behaving confidently if certainty is high and uncertainty low. So the more familiar and prescribed the situation, the better. Of course, despite the best-laid plans unexpected things will still happen, which is why a combination of techniques for the person and modifications to the situation is useful.

Slapdash

Slapdash people do things in a carelessly hasty way and are therefore inclined to make a lot of mistakes. Far from being mortified when mistakes come to light, they tend to shrug their shoulders, wonder what the fuss is about and continue in their slapdash ways. They have an irrepressible faith in their own ability and a low regard for attention to detail and quality, both of which they find tedious and boring.

The extent to which slapdash work is a problem depends on the responsibilities of the person concerned. If they do the sort of work that requires inspirational, broad-brush bursts of creativity, where other people are responsible for honing and polishing the finished article, then it may present no problem; on the contrary it might be an asset. If, on the other hand, attention to detail is the order of the day then the tendency to be slapdash is likely to be a serious handicap.

THE OPTIONS

▶ Do nothing

Left to their own devices the behaviour of slapdash people will be dictated by a strong preference to be hasty and leave others to attend to the details. If you do nothing, they will continue to assume that 'it will be all right on the night', and to avoid taking responsibility for the quality of their work.

▶ Alter your perception of the problem

You could perceive slapdash people as being gifted, right-brained creative types who perform best when unfettered by the burdens of detail. They simply operate on a different plane and have probably missed their true vocation as modern expressionist painters (the sort who throw paint at large canvasses and then ride bicycles over them!).

This may help you to see how to use them in a more creative capacity. It would certainly be worth checking whether they are natural lateral thinkers, able to make unusual connections between previously unrelated ideas.

Another possibility is to perceive some slapdash people as dyslexic, with a blind spot for words or numbers. Try as they might, their written work remains relatively disorganised, untidy, riddled with spelling mistakes and the like. Dyslexic people are bright and conscientious and usually excel orally and spatially. Again, this means that they are best equipped to do work that depends on speaking, drawing and keyboard skills rather than writing.

▶ Persuade the problem person to change

Slapdash people need to be encouraged to slow down and take responsibility for the quality to their work. Obviously they will not relish the prospect of being more painstaking, and their 'natural' inclination may always be to dash things off quickly on the back of an envelope. It is possible, however, to get them to accept that slapdash work, however inspired, is unacceptable as the finished product. You could concede that it may be appropriate in the early stages, when first mapping out a

169

piece of work, and in the first flushes of enthusiasm. So you are not persuading them never under any circumstances to be slapdash, merely that it has its proper time and place in the scheme of things, and that finished articles are not the proper time.

Your best bet is to agree precise quality standards for their work so that there are no differences in perception about what is acceptable. Standards could cover the legibility of handwriting, the accuracy of figure work, an acceptable level of spelling or grammatical mistakes, the thoroughness with which a case has been argued, the extent to which both sides of an argument have been put, whether there is a one-page summary giving the salient points and so on. Clearly the standards must be tailor-made to fit the nature of the work and the circumstances in which it is produced.

Once agreed, quality standards make it easier for the slapdash person to monitor their own work against the standards and, as a consequence, to take responsibility for quality. This is an example of the 'measure it and it improves' school of thought. Interestingly, the very act of pinning someone down and getting them to articulate precise measurable standards is in itself an excellent antidote to the tendency to be slapdash; defining standards demands care with words and an almost pedantic attention to detail.

▶ Modify the situation

Slapdash people have learned to be slapdash because on countless previous occasions they have got away with it. The joys of being slapdash have greatly exceeded any penalties or inconveniences. The situation needs to be modified so that this state of affairs is revised by ensuring that work which meets quality standards leads to 'nice' consequences and work which doesn't leads to 'nasty' consequences. 'Nasty' consequences might be having to correct the work (it is essential that no one else makes the corrections, since this is the equivalent of letting the slapdash person off the hook once again), or being 'punished' by having to do more, not less, detailed work. By contrast, when work meets the agreed quality standards they would be praised or given some kind of bonus, such as tackling a more creative piece of work which is more conducive to their style.

Providing the rewards and punishments are contingent upon the quality of work produced, this approach will gradually cause slapdash work to decrease and quality work to increase. Do not expect miracles or a sudden overnight transformation. Slapdash habits are acquired over a long period and they take time to be unlearned and replaced with something more punctilious.

Tactless

Tactless people say things that are discourteous and give offence. They tend to be off-hand and inconsiderate rather than setting out to be rude or insulting. Tactless remarks spring from a lack of sensitivity about people's feelings. If, for example, someone has recently suffered a bereavement, a tactless person will unthinkingly tell a joke about a mortuary. Or if someone is enormously overweight, a tactless person will draw attention to the notice in the lift restricting the number of occupants. Tactless remarks are inappropriate because they fail to take account of people's 'soft spots'.

Tactlessness is a problem because it often causes unnecessary offence and upset. Some situations are more sensitive than others but tactless people seem to have an uncanny knack of putting their foot in it regardless. The seriousness of the problem clearly depends on who takes offence and the extent to which they do so. If it is a customer, a sale could be lost. If it is a colleague, relations could be strained. If it is a subordinate, their enthusiasm could take a knock.

THE OPTIONS

▶ Do nothing

Ignoring tactless remarks leaves the tactless person in blissful ignorance and prone, therefore, to continue to cause offence inadvertently. Sometimes tactless people know themselves immediately after they have made a remark that it was inappropriate and, in their embarrassment and confusion, are quite likely to compound the problem by blurting out other ill-considered things. If they know only too well that they have put their foot in it, doing something to correct the situation is less important than if the tactless person remains blissfully unaware. Generally speaking, however, tactlessness is a behaviour we can do without and, if it persists, it behoves us to do something about it.

▶ Alter your perception of the problem

You could see tactless people as wide-eyed innocents who are uninhibited and say whatever comes into their minds. If you are surrounded by scheming, devious, diplomatic people, a tactless person could be something of a refreshing change. It is rare to have people who are so naive that they 'tell it the way it is' without choosing their words carefully and having ulterior motives.

Tactless remarks do not of themselves cause offence, for it depends on how the remark is received. It is possible to shrug tactlessness off as inconsequential or even to find it amusingly gauche. This perception could help you to tolerate the occasional tactless remark as a price worth paying in exchange for straightforward honesty.

▶ Persuade the problem person to change

The line you take depends on whether or not the person is aware of the offence caused. If they are self-aware and, having made a tactless remark, recognise and regret it, then counsel them to think before, rather than after, speaking. A practical plan might be to urge heavy censorship of all impromptu, off-the-cuff remarks. This is when tactless people are most likely to succumb and blurt something out that they immediately regret. When this happens, work out what could be done to limit the damage. A swift admission of tactlessness and an apology will often go a long way to saving the day. A succinct 'I'm sorry, that was tactless of me' will suffice. Anything longer makes it likely that they will exacerbate the situation and dig themselves in even deeper.

Tactless people who are unaware of the problem are more difficult to help. The fact that they are oblivious suggests that they are sufficiently thick-skinned either not to sense resentment in others or to blame other people for being over-sensitive and 'getting the wrong end of the stick'. The first step is to get them to distinguish between the tactless and the benign. As ever, some specific and recent examples are a powerful illustration. The second step is to to work out how they can do a bit of self-regulation. For example, you could encourage them to err on the side of assuming that everyone they meet is feeling vulnerable, unsure of themselves and ultra-sensitive. This won't always be true of course, but as an operating assumption it will do no harm and give useful practice in acquiring empathy. The ability to see things from the other person's point of view is a skill conspicuously absent in tactless people.

Realistically you must accept that the probability of transforming a tactless person into a diplomat is about as likely as making a silk purse out of a sow's ear, but at least you can coach them to the stage of not being tactless. The Book of Ecclesiastes has got it about right when it urges, 'And weigh thy words in a balance and make a door and bar for thy mouth.'

▶ Modify the situation

Unless they set out deliberately to be rude, tactless people are inclined to be tactless when they are in a situation where they are on the edge of their competence and feel out of their depth. It is the combination of a tricky situation and the opportunity to make impromptu remarks that triggers tactlessness. The answer is to minimise the occurrence of such situations either by confining the person to familiar situations well within their spheres of competence or by ensuring that they are well prepared. Even a careful plan can, of course, be upset by unexpected events, leaving the tactless person exposed and vulnerable. When this happens, you must step into the breach and not allow them to extemporise.

All this may sound heavily restrictive and protectionist, but keeping a tactless person well within their comfort zone is a necessary first step. Subsequently, as they put their foot in it less, the controls can be relaxed; but this should be phased and not sudden.

Temperamental

Temperamental people are liable to rapid and intense changes of mood. The changes can take various forms; they can become peevish and prickly or sullen and surly or grumpy and short-tempered. Temperamental people are touchy and quick to take offence. They are the sort of people who have wafer-thin skins and take umbrage at things thicker-skinned people wouldn't even notice.

Prickly people are a problem because they have a devastating effect on the openness and honesty of people around them. Normal straightforwardness is toned down for fear of provoking 'a mood'. People lean over backwards not to say anything that might cause offence. The 'kid gloves' treatment is exaggerated if the temperamental person is senior. Quite understandably subordinates attempt to reduce the swings of mood by heavily censoring anything resembling bad news. The effort invested in keeping the layers of the cocoon intact saps energy, wastes time and creates a dishonest atmosphere where, at the very least, people are economical with the truth.

THE OPTIONS

▶ **Do nothing**

If you do nothing, moodiness will remain undiminished. Moody people tend to assume that their temperament is beyond their control and that external events and happenings make them moody. They therefore view themselves as innocent victims of events, with no responsibility for their moods. All this makes it unlikely that they will ever effect a change themselves. You must do something to help them.

▶ **Change your perception of the problem**

You could view temperamental people as being refreshingly open about their emotions. They are the sort of people who wear their heart on their sleeve and leave you in no doubt about how they are feeling. Compare this with all the 'slow burn' people who suppress their feelings and amaze you when some apparently trivial event suddenly causes them to flip. Temperamental people show their feelings as they go along in much the same way that a barometer shows changes in atmospheric pressure. In this sense they are easier to read than apathetic people (see **Apathetic**). Temperamental people are often colourful characters who, while we may not relish many of their moods, certainly make life more interesting!

▶ **Persuade the problem person to change**

This is easier said than done with a temperamental person because of their utter conviction that their moods just happen as a reaction to external events beyond their control. There is no point in trying to persuade someone to control their moods if they don't accept that such a thing is possible. The best hope is to put your energy into getting them to see that they *choose* how they feel. This can be done by using a recent example where, even though something happened that usually provokes a mood, they took it in their stride. Any variation in their reaction will serve to demonstrate that they do not inevitably have to react temperamentally. Getting them to accept that they have a range of different reactions to what is ostensibly the same event, is the start of the realisation that they decide, not the situation. From these first dawnings they can be helped to take responsibility for their moods. This does not mean that they will never again be temperamental but at least, when they are, they can see that they have *chosen* to be moody. If you couple this with some adjustments to the situation (see below) you could have the problem cracked.

▶ Modify the situation

Temperamental people don't decide to be temperamental in a vacuum; something always happens to bring on their moods. What's more, they have 'discovered' from countless experiences that being temperamental gets them what they want, not necessarily every time, but often enough. Possible triggers for temperamental behaviour depend on the form it takes; triggers for prickly behaviour will differ from those for sullen behaviour. Generally speaking, however, triggers for sudden changes of mood are likely to be when:

- something inconvenient happens
- the person is asked to do something again or correct errors
- they are expected to do something out of the ordinary or beyond the call of duty
- they are slighted, overlooked, ignored or insulted.

Triggers such as these are, of course, inevitable in anything other than a sanitised environment. They are simply part of life's rich tapestry and it is unlikely that they can or should be avoided.

The real key to solving temperamental behaviour lies in changing the payoffs so that temperamental displays no longer 'work' for the problem person.

Typical payoffs for temperamental behaviour are that:

- people rally round and help with whatever has inconvenienced the problem person
- people 'lay off' the problem person and give them an easier time.
- people apologise for causing the upset.

These payoffs, and others like them, help us to see that, from the temperamental person's point of view, moody displays let them off the hook and give them an easier time. The cure is therefore to reverse the process and step up the pressure when they are temperamental and reduce it when they are not. Over a number of repetitions this teaches them that being temperamental does not pay. It helps if it is possible to tell them in advance that this is going to be your strategy. They won't like it, and may even try a mood to show you the error of your ways, but if you stick to the plan and deprive them of their payoffs the temperamental displays will decrease.

Two-faced

Two-faced people say one thing to your face and something else behind your back. They make ingratiating remarks to you but criticise you to other people and vice versa. They indulge in this duplicity in the belief that it wins them popularity and keeps everyone happy. In the short term their deceit may go undetected, but eventually people get to compare notes and when they don't add up the insincerity and hypocrisy of the two-faced person is exposed. An extraordinary characteristic of two-faced people is that they can never bring themselves to believe that their cover has been blown. So they carry on being deceitful, in the words of an old pop song, 'never saying what they mean, never meaning what they say', convinced that they are fooling most of the people most of the time.

Two-faced people are a problem because nothing they say can be taken at face value. Even when their praises are genuine you doubt that they can be. This mistrust fuels suspicion and causes people to spend inordinate amounts of time comparing notes and discovering inconsistencies.

THE OPTIONS

▶ Do nothing

If you opt to do nothing, two-faced behaviour will continue unabated and may even spread. Each time you apparently agree with a two-faced person you are, in effect, being two-faced yourself. If everyone opts for this, the easy way out, then two-facedness is being condoned and insidiously it takes a hold and becomes a way of life.

▶ Change your perception of the problem

You could be really charitable and perceive the two-faced person as well-meaning, anxious not to upset anybody and keen to promote harmony. The fact that they are blind to the possibility of being rumbled rather adds to the image of naive ineptitude.

The less charitable perception is that two-faced people are cowards who lack the courage to say what they really think and go to great lengths to avoid confrontation. They hope to have the best of both worlds; to get other people to do their dirty work for them and to remain the good guys. This perception may help you become more determined to call their bluff and expose them as double agents.

▶ Persuade the problem person to change

Two-faced people can best be helped to learn the error of their ways if you grasp the nettle and confront the problem. Of course they will find this an uncomfortable process because confrontations are exactly what they seek to avoid. Have to hand some chapter-and-verse examples of their duplicity and demonstrate how it no longer achieves the objective of keeping everyone happy. Explain that people have fallen into the habit of pooling their knowledge and checking for inconsistencies. The game is up; they are exposed.

It is unlikely that this shock tactic will provide a lasting solution to the problem. As the effect wears off, it is highly likely that the two-faced person will revert. Exhortation needs to be backed up with changes to the situation designed to help make a permanent adjustment.

▶ Modify the situation

Two-faced behaviour is most prevalent in 'off-the-record' one-to-one encounters with no witnesses. An obvious tactic is, therefore, to avoid one-to-one meetings with the two-faced person. There is safety in numbers and clearly the opportunities to make snide remarks about someone behind their back are much reduced if the someone is present. At least take the precaution of having a witness with you so that the person is more guarded and circumspect.

When you meet the two-faced person alone there are at least three things you can do to cramp their style. First, always make copious notes and do this quite openly. Two-faced people don't like notes; it makes the interaction seem more formal, more on the record. (Of course the ultimate deterrent would be an audio recorder but you are unlikely to be able to slap one of those down on the desk.)

Secondly, when they say something ingratiating which you know contradicts a view they have expressed to someone else say, 'As I understand it, that isn't what you said to so and so.' They'll deny the duplicity, but if you keep plugging away with this exposure *every single time* you catch them being hypocritical, it will gradually have the desired effect.

Thirdly, whenever they start to run someone down in your presence, refuse to continue with the conversation. Say, 'I'm sorry, but I don't want to discuss so and so unless they are present to defend themselves. Let's change the subject.'

The more people adopt these spoiling tactics the more the opportunities for two-faced behaviour are restricted.

Vague

Vague people are imprecise and hard to pin down. They leave things up in the air, with hazy pronouncements that fail to convey who is supposed to do what. Their conversations are littered with phrases that avoid or fudge the issue such as 'It depends'; 'We'll come back to that', 'As appropriate'; 'I'll leave you to tie up the details'; 'We all know what we mean'; and 'I'm sure we all understand what has to be done.' These last two are said when nothing could be further from the truth.

Vagueness is a problem because it violates your right to be clear. Some people relish the opportunity to exploit the loop-holes. Others find the ambiguity unnerving. If you fall into the latter category then you've got a problem. Of course, it's tempting to blame the vague person for being a poor communicator; surely the onus is on the transmitter not the receiver? This, however, leaves you confused but disinclined to do anything to improve the situation.

THE OPTIONS

▶ Do nothing

This is not recommended, unless you can exploit the vagueness and use to advantage the room for manoeuvre it unintentionally provides. Otherwise if you do nothing, airy-fairy vagueness is bound to continue unabated.

▶ Alter your perception of the problem

You could regard the vague person as someone who is leaning over backwards to accommodate everybody and maximise the likelihood of agreement. It is easier for people to agree to something broad and all-embracing (affectionately called by some 'motherhood and apple pie') than to something detailed and specific. This sort of agreement is, however, often more apparent than real. Vague statements are open to different interpretations, so people end up agreeing to different things without necessarily realising it. This is why communiques at the conclusion of international conferences so often lapse into generalities; the words are left vague to allow for as much broad agreement as possible. So you could come to see your vague person as a promoter of harmony and agreement; someone who is anxious to avoid conflict and aggravation. Unfortunately vagueness is the equivalent of papering over the cracks in that it temporarily gives the impression that all is well but underneath the tranquil surface the cracks continue to open up.

▶ Persuade the problem person to change

Vagueness and fudging are habits people develop over time. It is unlikely to be particularly conscious or deliberate, so raising it as an issue is likely to be something of a shock to the vague person. The last thing you want is for them to retreat into vagueness as a defence against what they may construe as a hostile attack! Be gentle with them. Don't accuse them of being a poor communicator, but admit that you are often unclear or slow on the uptake and would prefer to have things spelled out in more detail. It then becomes a need you have rather than a criticism.

It is unlikely that this request for specifics will be sufficient to solve the problem. It is predictable that left to their own devices, vague people will continue to fudge the issue. They need the support of changed circumstances to bring about a lasting behaviour change.

▶ Modify the situation

There are at least three things you can do to modify the situation and pressurise the problem person to communicate with greater precision.

First, when things are vague you can take it upon yourself to ask questions of clarification. People are often reluctant to do this for fear of appearing stupid or slow, but when you are not clear you are safe in assuming that someone else isn't either. When you are brave enough to seek clarification in meetings, you will invariably find other people join in or are appreciative that you took the initiative.

Secondly, you can take it upon yourself to test your understanding by offering a detailed summary. You simply say, in your own words, your precise understanding of what has been said. This forces the vague person to correct or confirm your summary and in so doing, to dot the i's and cross the t's. A spin-off is that you get practice in summarising, which is a useful skill in many situations.

Thirdly, you could adopt an assumptive approach. When something is vague and you have room for manoeuvre, assume that you have the authority to do something unless someone specifically says you haven't. An excellent way to test the limits of your authority is to give notice *in writing* that you are going ahead with a particular action on a specified date and do so unless you are told not to. This tends to bring things to a head and, if your proposed action is stopped, you are owed an explanation which will force the vague person off the fence.

In all three cases your own behaviour has been the means of modifying the vagueness. Changing your approach obviates the need to persuade, counsel or remonstrate with the vague person and is more likely to solve your problem.

Whinger

People who whinge have got grumbling down to a fine art. They are given to whining and moaning about the things that happen to them. Their basic philosophy is that life should always be fair and when it isn't (which is most of the time) they whinge. They moan because other people are paid more than they are, have a better working environment and resources, have a fairer boss, have more cooperative colleagues, have a better bus service and so on and so on. Despite the fact that life is patently not fair, and that nobody ever said it would be, whingers hang on to their basic belief that it *should* be. This means that whenever there is a disparity between what they believe should happen and what actually happens, they are upset and whinge

Whinging is a problem because it is infectious; it rapidly takes a hold and reduces people's morale. Whole conversations between people can amount to one long moan. It is invariably unproductive, however, for it is rare for whingers to take any initiative to improve the situation. If they did, they might run out of things to grumble about and that would never do! It's always up to other people, 'them' as opposed to 'us', to do something to correct the supposed injustice.

THE OPTIONS

▶ **Do nothing**

It is easy to get used to whinging (you can get used to anything!) and accept it as the norm. Grumbling is, however, never in itself productive, so doing nothing condones a behaviour which is time-consuming and provides no added value. It is preferable to do something either to ensure that grumbling is a prelude to action or to contain it.

▶ **Alter your perception of the problem**

You could regard whingers as the custodians of fair play. Since they persist in believing that the world should be fair you could come to see them as an invaluable test of fairness. You could then instigate griping sessions where you listened to all the injustices, defended nothing, and went away wiser to reflect on what, if anything, should be done.

Alternatively you could perceive whingers as agents of change. All changes start with someone feeling dissatisfied with the status quo and with a vision of how much better things could be. This creates a tension for change, which is a positive desire to do something to improve the situation. So whingers, with all their dissatisfactions, are halfway there; they are useful people who are never satisfied. If they could be helped to do the other half and generate ideas, whingers would be a positive force for change.

▶ **Persuade the problem person to change**

There is no point in trying to persuade a habitual whinger that they should give it up because they are likely to be adamant that the gods are on their side. A much better idea is to get them to see the inefficiency of merely grumbling and the advantages of pushing things that bit further by making suggestions for improvement. Agree a formula whereby for every two gripes, they have to produce at least one recommendation. A ratio of one to one would be even better but you could be more reasonable to start with. The advantage of this plan is that grumbling becomes a means to an end rather than an end in itself. Each whinge is, in effect, a springboard for action.

As whingers take their first faltering steps towards producing recommendations you will notice that they are always things for other people to do. Gradually you could encourage them to implicate themselves by asking 'And what are *you* going to do to improve the situation?' With patience you will convert a whinger into a suggester and a suggester into a doer.

▶ Modify the situation

No one was born whinging (though babies that cry a lot give a very good imitation); they learned to do it as a means of winning sympathy. Triggers for whinging are when:

- inequitable treatment has been meted out
- a sympathetic person is available to listen
- the whinger feels powerless, an innocent victim of events outside their control.

Payoffs for whingers are that:

- people listen sympathetically
- the whinger feels better (a problem shared is a problem halved)
- they prove that someone else is to blame or needs to correct the situation
- something is done to improve the situation

These triggers and payoffs reinforce the wisdom of calling the whinger's bluff and pressurising them to take responsibility for suggesting improvement and for part of the action. By putting the monkey firmly back on their shoulder you have shown them that whinging is but a fraction of the story.

Workaholic

Workaholics are compulsive workers. They over-commit themselves through a deep-seated conviction that they are indispensible. They are sure that everything will grind to a halt without them. Workaholics work long hours. They pride themselves on getting to work before, and staying later than, anyone else. Sixteen-hour days and taking work home at weekends are the norm. Relaxation is a dirty word to a workaholic. If they go on holiday, they tend to keep active and fret about what is happening (or not happening!) in their absence. Frequent phone calls back to base keep them up to date with events and remind people of their existence.

Workaholics are a problem because they assume that everyone should be working just as hard as they do. If someone goes home on time they are immediately branded as a slacker. Unreasonable demands are placed on people: breakfast meetings, lunch 'on the hoof' and never leaving the office before eight in the evening all become accepted custom and practice. A highly competitive, 'macho' philosophy rapidly takes hold that separates the men from the boys purely on the basis of the number of hours worked. No one dares break the mould for fear of being branded a wimp. Workaholics are fond of taking a tough line and saying things like 'If you can't stand the heat, get out of the kitchen.'

THE OPTIONS

▶ **Do nothing**

If you do nothing to combat the workaholic's compulsion to work, it is inevitable that the problem will remain and become even more entrenched. The best you can hope for is some momentous event that will cause them to reappraise their priorities. A heart attack might do the trick or some other trauma that gets them to put their work into perspective and balance it with other commitments.

▶ **Alter your perception of the problem**

You could view workaholics in two different ways: either as conscientious people with too much to do, or as enthusiasts who love their work and have no desire to do anything else. Both these perceptions may leave you wishing that there were more workaholics around; if you are surrounded by lazy minimalists (see **Lazy**) you would presumably be delighted to swop them for a few conscientious enthusiasts!

The trouble with workaholics as we have seen, is that, since no man is an island, they cannot be contained. Other people are expected to subjugate their priorities and fall in line with the workaholic's. This puts unacceptable pressure on people, who may well be quietly efficient, to conform or else.

▶ **Persuade the problem person to change**

Workaholics who love their work are notoriously difficult people to influence. If they live to work, why on earth should they do less and risk undermining the very purpose of their existence? The mistake with such people is to attempt to persuade them to do less and thereby create a void. Voids are very threatening to workaholics, and when they come across one they immediately set to work to fill it with activity. A more constructive approach is to persuade them to extend their energies to a broader range of activities. They need *more* enthusiasms, not less, so that work is not the be-all and end-all. Encourage them to get involved with a deserving charity or to become a world authority on something (and write a book about it!).

Workaholics whose work is never done, and who choose to feel guilty if they are not working, need a different approach. They need to be persuaded to prioritise more rigorously. The chances are that they are failing to distinguish between tasks that are urgent and important and those that are urgent but not important and important but not urgent. (Really bad cases may even be putting the non-urgent and unimportant jobs in the same bracket as the urgent and important ones.) Redefined priorities are the key to getting the over-conscientious workaholic to see what to do (the urgent and important), what to delegate (the urgent and unimportant), what to plan (the non-urgent but important) and what not to do (the non-urgent and unimportant).

Rigorous prioritising also helps the workaholic to say 'No' with justification and, eventually, without guilt.

▶ **Modify the situation**

Workaholism is fuelled by strong inner compulsions, but there are a number of things you could do to alleviate the problems it causes.

The enthusiastic workaholic, with an insatiable appetite for work, should be given more and more to do. The tasks should be preferably of the top secret 'for your eyes only' variety so that the workaholic is prevented from making everyone else's life a misery. Eventually even the most hardened workaholic will protest that they have more than their fair share of work.

The over-committed workaholic, with a never-ending stream of work, should only be allocated tasks on a drip-feed 'complete this before you get the next' basis. If their work can be channelled in this way it builds in clear completion points and regulates the flow of work so that the necessity to work during evenings and weekends is avoided.

The other way to improve the situation is to ring-fence the workaholic so that he or she inflicts the minimum amount of suffering on other people. The more the workaholic can be kept beavering away in relative isolation, the better for all concerned.

Worrier

Worriers fret about things that might happen; often they don't but that doesn't prevent worriers from worrying. Worriers share some of the characteristics of pessimists (see **Pessimist**) in that their basic philosophy is 'If something can go wrong it will.' The difference is that pessimists are confident that the worst will happen whereas worriers fear that the worst might happen. If you expect the worst you are gloomy but resigned to the inevitable. If, on the other hand, you are in a state of uncertainty, you are likely to become agitated, nervous and on edge while you wait for an outcome.

For a habitual worrier, worrying is a familiar but unpleasant emotion that spills over into outward behaviour. Among the tell-tale signs are:

- an inability to concentrate on the 'here-and-now'
- fussing and fiddling with small, insignificant things
- a preoccupation with the 'terrible' things that might happen
- not sleeping properly.

All these behaviours have an adverse effect on the worrier's performance. Other people can also be distracted by their preoccupations.

THE OPTIONS

▶ **Do nothing**

If you ignore the worriers they will carry on fretting but at least it might not be so obvious. Accomplished worriers are quite capable of suppressing their feelings so that their behaviours are not too twitchy. If you are a hard-liner you might argue that people's emotions are beyond your jurisdiction and no concern of yours; all you care about is their performance – their behaviour. While ultimately this is true, if you know someone to be a worrier, it is more helpful to acknowledge it and attempt to help rather than to leave them to stew.

▶ **Alter your perception of the problem**

You could see worrying as a sign that someone is conscientious and caring. After all, if people couldn't care less they are immune to worry. People who worry want things to turn out well but are anxious that they might not. It is the 'iffiness' that worries them. An appropriate level of concern is obviously welcome as an enhancement to performance. The problem with worry is that it goes well beyond concern and is superfluous to requirements. We need to see how to retain the conscientiousness but alleviate the worry.

▶ **Persuade the problem person to change**

Telling someone not to worry has no effect whatsoever, other than to risk encouraging them to worry about the fact that they are worried! Worriers rarely need convincing that worrying doesn't change anything. If they do need to be convinced of this get them to consider the week ahead on a Monday, and list all the things they are worried about, then to look back over the week on the Friday and with hindsight list all the things they should have worried about. A comparison of the Monday and Friday lists usually reveals considerable dissimilarities, thus apparently proving the futility of worrying. Unfortunately determined worriers will not consider this convincing proof because they will rationalise that things turned out well because they worried and things turned out less well because they didn't worry!

Most worriers already accept that worrying doesn't help, but are adamant that they are powerless to control their feelings. Your task is to get them to accept that they *choose* to worry in certain situations and could equally well choose to feel concerned rather than worried. The distinction is one they will need help with. The crucial difference is that concerned people take action, whereas worried people are immobilised and just worry. It is unrealistic to expect to convert a worrier into a slap-happy, carefree, laid-back person but it is realistic to get them to tone down their worrying so that it becomes concern.

Since action is the best antidote to worry, the most fruitful line to take is to get them to combat worry as a three-stage process. First, when they are next worried they should write down a description of the outcome they fear most. Secondly, they should assume that this will definitely happen. Thirdly, they should answer the question 'Is there anything I can do right now to prevent this happening?' If the answer is yes, do it. If the answer is no, go and do something else. Each step in this approach helps to alleviate worry; writing down the fear makes it official; assuming it will happen removes any doubts; and doing something is better than being immobilised.

▶ Modify the situation

Worriers have learned to worry; no one was born worrying. Even the most practised worriers do not worry all the time. Certain situations tend to send them off down the familiar slippery slope. Invariably they have favourite topics that are the focus of their worries, such as health and safety, financial security, making a good impression or winning approval. The irony is that the more they worry about such things the more they jeopardise them.

There is nothing you can do to the situation that will inevitably *make* people not worry (any more than there are things you can do to make them worry). As we have seen, they and they alone choose whether or not to worry. However, there are things you can do to distract them from worrying. For example, you could keep them busy with tasks to do against a tight deadline. The best activities are absorbing ones that require thought and concentration. If idle hands make the most mischief, it's idle brains that do the most worrying.

When someone admits that they are worried, or you can detect that they are from their outward behaviour, it is best to acknowledge it sympathetically and ask 'What are you going to do about it?' This makes it clear that the responsibility lies with them and gently goads them into action, with all the advantages we saw earlier.

Index